UGLY DUCKLING PRESSE :: DOSSIER

Apart
© 2012 Catherine Taylor

ISBN: 978-1-933254-96-8

Cataloging-in-publication data is available from the Library of Congress.

Distributed to the trade by
Small Press Distribution
1341 Seventh Street, Berkeley, CA 94710
www.spdbooks.org

Available directly from UDP and through our partner bookstores:
www.uglyducklingpresse.org/orders
www.uglyducklingpresse.org/bookstores

This book is funded, in part, by an award from the National Endowment
for the Arts.

Images on pages 80-83, 123, 125-127, 139, and 143 used by permission
of the Black Sash Collection, Manuscripts and Archives Department,
University of Cape Town Libraries.

Image on page 82 used courtesy of Robin Trehaven.

First Edition 2012
Printed in the USA

Ugly Duckling Presse
The Old American Can Factory
232 Third Street #E-301
Brooklyn, NY 11215

www.uglyducklingpresse.org

NATIONAL
ENDOWMENT
FOR THE ARTS

CATHERINE TAYLOR APART

Contents

A person writes a sentence. The sentence is neither good nor bad, but poses its subject and predicate in the ordinary fashion. Maybe you, too, are sick of mediation, of words that get in the way of what you want to say.

—Wayne Koestenbaum

The starting point of critical elaboration is the consciousness of what one really is, and is "knowing thyself" as a product of the historical process to date which has deposited in you an infinity of traces, without leaving an inventory. Therefore, it is imperative at the outset to compile such an inventory.

—Antonio Gramsci

APART

Prologue: Forms of Parallel Transport

After it is over, after the shooting stops, after the blood bath, after things change, after democracy, after reconciliation, after redistribution, after understanding, maybe then it will begin.

See how the periodic sentence uses parallel phrases to withhold its essential element; marked by suspended syntax, it places its final revelation right before the concluding period.

Like the sentence, the people move forward, want resolution, seek conclusions, note parallels, but they, of course, reach no final revelations, no concluding periods—no time with an end, no discrete clause of history, no full stop.

A period is an interval of time in a cyclic motion; a period is determined by recurring phenomena.

(Listen.) Even a sentence can seem like a pendulum.

A period is an interval of time in a cyclic motion; a period is determined by recurring phenomena.

To start with this or that. Once, my children and I made a science project: Foucault's pendulum. A squirt-bottle of black paint hung upside down from a rafter on a long string. Un-stopper the bottle, set the paint-bob swinging, watch the trail of paint inscribe the motion of the earth beneath you. In my notebooks from this time there are endless meditations on oscillation, on vacillation, on going back and forth in approaches to a topic, in modes of representation, in love. On being pulled between poles. Back and forth the notes swing between prose and verse, narrative and rupture, faith and doubt, black and white, change and stasis, self and other, amnesty and retribution, sound and silence, remembering and forgetting, colonialism and independence, poverty and wealth, belonging and alienation, alien and citizen, positivist documentary historiography and radical performative constructivism, sick with desire and sick of it. Back and forth.

But look at the line the world traces. The revelation of the system, of course, is that the pendulum doesn't just swing back and forth, between this or that, inscribing simple opposites. Instead, it leaves a trail of ever-shifting ellipses, each arc overlapping the last, but also moving on—all a single line that loops into a flower, describing, ultimately, in its center, a circle. Inside the circle flower words that trouble simple oppositions, words like discourse, ideology, blood, race, family, nation, history.

A complete swing of a pendulum is a period. What is periodic repeats itself.

A pendulum keeps time.

A pendulum is a harmonic oscillator. So is the human voice, and some stars. Usually, we cannot hear harmonics as separate notes; instead, they appear to be the timbre of the tone.

A pendulum exhibits resonance. It vibrates easily at particular frequencies, less so at others. An acoustically resonant object filters out all frequencies other than its resonance. In the telling of histories, what if nothing is filtered? Will we hear only noise or everything resonating at once?[1]

Resonance is produced by sympathetic vibrations. Resonance evokes associations and emotions.

Resonance can result in catastrophic failure of the vibrating structure. This is known as "resonance disaster." (Soldiers, break step.) Look how we have learned to love the wreckage.

I. Cape Town Journals

Cape Town Flower Market

A jet-lag dreaminess. White arum lilies twist above their three-foot stalks. Bunches, circumferences big as tree trunks. Papery red poppies with bent hairy stems. Irises. Sick visual abundance. Colored women man the stalls. Across the sidewalk, a single black man sells knit caps and radios.

One flower-seller asks, *Did you come to see the new South Africa?* Some mocking sound in her voice. Yes, my mother grew up here, emigrated. I visited as a child, until '76, Soweto, I haven't been back since then. A laugh. *Coming for some "truth and reconciliation"? Huh. Truth is it's much worse now. At least for us coloreds.* More crime, worse schools, no jobs. There's no "liberation."

Don't listen to her! The guy across the way yells. We have democracy now! *Hah! Democracy. Good for the blacks. Used to be whites on top, us in the middle, and blacks on the bottom. Now black's on top and we're on the bottom.* No. He says no. We are all black.

I nod my head; this seems like a good slogan. I'm getting ready to raise my little white black power fist in the air when, without hesitating, she says, *Oh. How about we're all colored?* A gesture at the three of us: black, white, colored. *We are all colored.* Why not? The mix, the creole, "mestiza consciousness." He looks away and hesitates. She says, *No? How about we're all white?* He closes his mouth and frowns. Doesn't respond. *See. We can all be black, but not all colored or all white.*

I nod more slowly as the categories unravel and resolidify. The power of claiming black clear for him and maybe for her, but troubling when it comes to white me. He says, (No. All black. *Because he doesn't want to give up the power. It's about power.*) He shakes his head, no. *They're just switching apartheid.* Okay, okay. We are all the same. *Okay. All the same. All colored.* He shakes his head, no.

They are at an impasse.

He says to me, She's crazy, it's much better now. He backs away from the questions of race, nation, power, and identity she has raised. When he calls her crazy, I feel my allegiance shifting away from him, a gendered history tugging me to her.

She hands me my flowers wrapped in white paper and I think she is a brilliant political philosopher and rhetorician. But then, his insistence on both his and "our" blackness, his refusal to take in any whiteness, and his ultimate retreat from our mutual search for a common name make sense in terms of power and a politics of difference. Still, confusion blooms.

[handwritten left margin: all black: "all have power" but isn't true]

[handwritten: apartheid: laws that established seperate areas/facilities/homelands (similar to indian reservations) for whites and blacks similar to Jim Crow laws]

(in time, confusion's nearly constant, or at least recurs, a lunar phase
where absence is illusion and sequence limns some consolation.)
To chart this fluid oscillation will take both story and aphasia.
To say, *if I were him*, at once irreverent and divine. How can we
disavow the godlike while still kneeling for the gesture? Can I
convince you of my blindness with my lemony vision? Give me
the time called chirotic, outside chronology, in front of the unknown, where explanations break down, where experience is real.
A time of documents and a longing for redemption. Then soak
your kites in kerosene and let me be clear,(this story twists on
the stake of me and mine.) Or leave that all behind and consider
forgiveness (rhetorical or real) as we break through the clouds.

*After apartheid ended, one deal was there would be no mass persecution of people who held up apartheid

*aphasia creates choppy thoughts

*Pulled in two directions

*confusion: relates to lost sentence of story

*I don't consider other people that are different

*can she prove her point since in wasn't the norm

*relates to her experience

*how her experience ties to the country

*reconciliation

-17-

Arrivals

The airport gleams glassy in the blue and yellow morning light. Travelers to Cape Town drift through a windowed aerial corridor, still swooning from their dawn view of Africa's lovely tapered end of land with its empty beaches and crashing ocean, Table Mountain lumbering above the city hurled against it. The passport area is an expansive glass box that says here you are, with all the clean modern romance of travel and all the lure of Africa safely presented for your consumption.

Just beyond the uniformed stamp-stamp of the customs agents, small digital billboards glow with shots of red Kalahari sunsets and yellow lions' eyes. Everything is orderly. Everything is spotless. For tourists, all this will reappear in the sparkling windows of a hotel overlooking the waterfront where luxury catamarans sail out for an afternoon of Table Mountain views and fine wines. Later, they'll visit gracious, white Cape mansions filled with Dutch East India booty, and, maybe the next day, fly to a game reserve where fresh impala is served under the stars before retiring to linen sheets in an elegant tent on its platform of rare wood.

But we're not there. There is one arrival and then there is another. We've got our bags and the car, but we still need to travel from the bauble of the airport to the jewel of the city. And the thread on which they are strung is known as The Hell Run, a 5-mile, six-lane swath through a series of black townships, a slice across a larger network of wood and tin shacks and tiny concrete houses that make up all of the Cape townships, home to over a million people. At the heart of this story is this little strip. This strip *is* the story. We're going to have to drive it. Some say to go hell-for-leather, pedal-to-the-metal, with the doors locked and no stopping for anything since the last attack was just a week ago. But we're going to have to stop and pull over—that's why we're here.

We are always looking for a route. A way in. A way through. And we always leave one behind. Look, there's Langa, where my mother was a social worker in 1959, where white police massacred dozens of residents in 1960, and more in 1980, and so many along the way of apartheid's systematic violence. There's Crossroads. Remember it? Black billows of tire smoke, military vehicles with young white security officers careening through the streets, shooting off a few rounds, jumping out and whipping their sjamboks into people, again and again. 1985, there and on TV, when dinner talk was of the coming bloodbath whites, in turn, would suffer. Look, there's Gugulethu where the Gugulethu Seven lay dead on the ground, and there's somebody feeding their baby just like, and not at all like, somebody before them. We are looking in from the outside. We are looking out from the inside. We are looking from the side of the road, taking pictures through the window. We are never going to get out of this car.

always inside inside a car. Even with the windows down, the fields and trees and people squatting in their yards are impossibly distant. Say, *the burning stump by the side of the road is still burning*. The children shift to watch it smoke over the split lip of the door. You are writing a letter in your head, a rubric of disavowal, at high speed, so you need to drive faster. The back seat lags behind you. The car might as well be a limousine with all that space back there. The letter you are writing spools out in loops and jags. The road gaps and buckles. Distantly, you hear the children say, *faster, faster.*

Three Planes

[T]he telling of the individual story and the individual experience cannot but ultimately involve the whole laborious telling of the collectivity itself.

—Fredric Jameson

Memory's not a movie, but there's a long black leader here. No soundtrack. Three planes.

The sun glints off plane number one's fuselage as it descends toward Paris, a stopover between New York and Cape Town. A silver shark descending.

Plane number two drops through a liquid night sky toward Africa.

Plane number three skids to a halt on the salt-spray tarmac of an island somewhere in the Atlantic.

PLANE NUMBER ONE

Paris. Outside the window, the air is gray. Slate roofs and faded asphalt pass below us. People in the plane are chatting and rustling. It is the late sixties and air travel still retains a hint of glamour. Glasses clink as young stewardesses in navy-blue caps and little silk neck scarves bend their stockinged legs and tuck their carts away for the landing. People put up their tray tables. Outside the window, we can see tiny cars. Little Renaults and Peugeots. The plane seesaws tipsily in the wind near the ground. The runway appears.

Suddenly, a cart of glasses crashes against the galley and we are on our backs, slammed against the seats, tilted now in an impossible angle, faces to the sky, as the plane pushes up, up into the air, a steep climb like a roller coaster, skyward. There is the sound of onboard luggage crashing into the backside of the bins. Outside the window, the massive bulk of another plane slips past right below us. In an impossible, but vivid, memory, faces appear in a row of bubble portals. In our plane, there is a collective gasp, a scream or two, and then silence. Except for one voice.

I am singing. Loudly, joyfully.

"The wheels on the bus go round and round. Round and round." I am four. My mother smiles and sings along quietly.

Slowly, people begin to talk again. There is some commotion. The captain comes on and apologizes in a clipped English accent.

My mother squeezes my hand. "Exciting!" she says. She dazzles with her smile.

Below us, the plane on the runway recedes, and an anecdote starts to form. At first, it is simply a story of danger and unawareness (*ignorance is bliss*). Later, it is synecdoche: below us, not just the plane on the runway. Below us, Paris in May '68. Below us, not just the streets full of little Renaults and Peugeots, but crowds of striking students and workers. Clouds of tear gas. The cars burned and stacked into barricades. Some streets barely there as the cobblestones were dug up to make more barricades or hurl at police. ("Under the paving stones, the beach.") The old social order crashing down.

Night over Africa. It is the early 1970s. Vietnam, Watergate, the massacre at the Munich Olympics, second grade.

In the plane, it is dim. Some passengers sleep, some read under miniature spotlights. Tiny gold and silver starbursts on the beige wall covering twinkle here and there. We are several hours into a thirteen-hour flight. We have settled in for the long haul. My mother has moved my younger brother and me to the rear of the plane where there is enough floor space to play with his battered fleet of Matchbox cars. Suddenly, the cabin lights come on and we hear the captain.

"I'm sorry to disturb you," he says, (that clipped accent), "but we will soon be making an unscheduled refueling stop in Entebbe, Uganda. All seat backs and tray tables must be in the upright position. Please prepare for descent."

We are descending rapidly as he speaks. Things are tipping. I know about Uganda. It is the home of Idi Amin. His face and military medals glisten in the news magazines on the coffee table at home. African independence struggles and scotch on the rocks.

The plane is only half full, so my mother moves my brother and me to empty seats in the nearby last row. The stewardess buckles herself into a seat across from us and begins to cry. My mother turns to look at her. "We're not low on fuel, are we?"

The stewardess shakes her head. No. "We've lost an engine," she tells my mother between little sobs.
My mother turns back to us and tightens the belts on our laps, pulling

up on the silver handle, snugging and smoothing the aqua-blue strap against our little hips. She smiles and says, "Do you remember the crash position?" I nod and show her, crossing my arms over my forehead and folding myself in half like a Swiss army knife, my long hair falling around my knees, down near the hem of my bell-bottom pants, down to my suede lace-ups. My brother hunches over next to me.

"Good job," my mother says. Then, with a smile, "This will be an adventure!" And with that, she undoes her own seatbelt, slips out into the aisle and goes to sit with the crying stewardess. She puts her arm around the woman and talks to her. I can't understand what they are saying.

I look at my brother, who is silently spinning the wheels of a tiny toy car with his index finger, and then I look out the window. I see my reflection, press my face against the pane, cup my hands around my eyes. Africa below is a field of black, like paint, like plastic. No lights, nothing to indicate how close to the ground we are. There is no warning. One minute we are flying, the plane tipping gently from side to side in the wind, and the next minute we are crashing into the ground. Our bodies fly forward, our seat belts jam into our stomachs, and all around us passengers are slamming their arms and heads into the seats in front of them. Many vomit simultaneously from the impact. My brother and I look at each other. Gross. For years, this was the part of the story we liked to tell best. Now, we are bumping along in a stubbled field.

After a while, we slow, stop, and get out into the thick, wet, warm air of Uganda. We walk toward the airport where we pass through a rain of dead bugs falling from an enormous, electric blue insect zapper mounted on a high pole. The bugs fizz, then tick and clatter on the concrete, crunch under our feet. Later, this will be our second favorite part of this story. The atmosphere. The rain of bugs.

I don't remember any fear of dying or the sick panic of imminent loss. My mother told us it was an adventure, and it was. Today, my favorite part of this story is that our mother flew us over and over again into the heart of history, into places where the world was changing, places of revolution we brushed past, aware and not aware. My brother will become an Air Force pilot. I will turn toward history.

PLANE NUMBER THREE

Skids to a halt on the salt-spray tarmac of an island somewhere in the Atlantic.

It is night. It is 1975. We are leaving South Africa for New York. Home. Next year, on June 16, Soweto's residents will rise up against the oppressive apartheid educational system and the South African government will respond by killing more than 700 people, including students and children. I don't know it now, but this will be my last visit for twenty-eight years. Events in Soweto will make it impossible to pretend it is okay to enjoy the privileges of white South Africa, impossible to pretend that nothing bad is happening, impossible to pretend that in visiting we aren't even more complicit with the apartheid regime than when we simply stay home.

Outside the window, the night world is black. Below us, much of Africa is in turmoil. It is a moment of transition, for some, from colonial rule to the exigencies of post-coloniality. A recent coup in Portugal is leading to independence for many of their African colonies. After years of fighting, Mozambique declared independence ten days ago. June 25, 1975. The victorious FRELIMO party announced Marxist rule under the leadership of Samora Machel (whose widow will later marry Nelson Mandela and become the only woman to have been the first lady of two nations). Despite independence, Mozambique will continue to fight a long and devastating war against a force of Rhodesian and then South African–supported contras known first as MNR then as RENAMO. UNICEF figures will later show that close to 500,000 children under the age of five will die between 1980 and 1988 alone from war-related causes. But right now, it is a time of celebration and of hope for black Mozambicans.

On the opposite coast, somewhere under our plane, in Angola, hopes are also rising. Independence will be achieved in the next few months. I imagine them celebrating.

Soundtrack: Angolan music from the '70s, the lilting slightly syncopated beat, twanging electric guitars, chiming acoustic ones, quick drums, the lead male voice in blurry Portuguese followed by a crowd of women responding. A traffic whistle bleats periodically.

But first, right now, in 1975, below this plane, the killing will intensify. Eventually, there will be close to half a million people dead over the course of a struggle that won't officially end for twenty-seven years, in 2002.

This month, South Africa will invade Angola. South Africa supports UNITA (led by Jonas Savimbi) and Zaire supports the FNLA in an uneasy alliance, one to which the CIA will give $14 million in the next few weeks, just as the Soviet Union and Cuba step up their support of Angola's Marxist liberation party, the MPLA (*Movimento Popular de Libertação de Angola*). The anti-colonial struggle is deeply enmeshed in global Cold War politics; both United States and South African involvement is supposed to be a secret.[2] Right now, beneath me, South African troops are massing on the border. Later, when I ask my cousin where he did his military service he'll say, "on the border." When I ask a relative years later what this meant, where exactly that was, he says, We hardly knew, we weren't supposed to know. But my cousin will be fighting down there soon, on the border. Or what South Africa called "the border," but Namibians call Namibia.

Namibia, the occupied territory formerly known as South-West Africa, lies between South Africa and Angola, but the Afrikaner government in Pretoria treats it as part of their nation, not recognizing its bid for independence. Here too, years of fighting. Here, South Africa's opposition is the Angola-based Namibian independence force, SWAPO (the South-West Africa People's Organization). Namibia's struggle will drag on. They won't become an independent nation until 1990. Fifteen years from now.

Now, we are flying home and have stopped to refuel on what my mother, when she tells this story, always calls "a rock in the middle of the Atlantic." As we taxi in, a tiny airport terminal comes into sight. It is draped in sheets covered with spray-painted words. We recognize this sign as political, but it is in a language we don't understand. Later, my mom says, "I think that place was called Isle de Sol."

The plane stops far from the building, and for what seems like a very long time, nothing happens. Then, a set of wheeled steps is pushed up and a group of beret-wearing soldiers with automatic weapons slung over their shoulders comes on board. Later, my mother says, "Maybe they were Portuguese? Or Angolan?" All passengers must disembark. As we pass through the plane's small oval portal, out into the windy island night, my mother, slim and elegant, pauses, one machine-gun carrying man on either side of her. She reaches nonchalantly into her pocketbook, takes out a deep blue silk scarf that whips and flutters in the wind, and ties it carefully over her dark, blowing hair. It is a gesture my brother and I have seen dozens of times, as familiar as the clink of the three thin gold bracelets she never seems to take off. As she reaches back to click the clasp of her bag, she says, quietly, "Whatever happens, don't give them your passports." Then she bends her knees a bit to reach our hands, and flashes her happiest smile, a smile that covers everything, and we smile back as she turns around, complicit in her spin.

Thirty years later, I look for Isle de Sol in the atlas, checking the index, checking off the coast of Angola, along the axis from South Africa to New York. I can't find it. I put it aside to research further later. Then, one day, I'm watching Chris Marker's film *Sans Soleil*. We hear the voice of the narrator. She says: "Every time he came back from Africa, he stopped at the island of Sal. Which is, in fact, a salt rock in the middle of the Atlantic."

A rock in the middle of the Atlantic. A tipping in my head; everything in my story slides down the shelf of memory. Sal? Is this where I was? Not Isle de Sol as I had always heard it, but Sal. The film continues: "Crews of transcontinental planes are rotated on Sal. Their club brings to this frontier of nothingness a small touch of the seaside resort which makes the rest still more unreal."

I rewind and watch the scene again. This looks like the place. And if it is, in fact, Ilha da Sal in the Cape Verde archipelago, those gun-toting guys certainly weren't Angolan, and probably not Portuguese, but troops of the revolutionary PAIGC, the combined forces of Cape Verde and Guinea-Bissau led first by Amilcar Cabral and then by his brother, Luiz. The PAIGC, FRELIMO, and the MPLA often worked together as CONCP (Conferencia das Organizacoes Nacionalistas das Colonias Portugesas). They gained their independence on July 5, 1975. I look back at the pictures of us in South Africa on that vacation. Me, eleven years old, wearing an alpaca poncho. Our South African Airways plane, refueling off its line of flight because other African countries were denying air passage rights to protest apartheid. Us, a version of the enemy, landing into their victory. The back of the pictures all say July, 1975.

The soundtrack here: morna, saudade, accordion, ache.

This is the story my mother tells about that trip: My brother went to the bathroom and when he flushed, the toilet gushed up instead of down, leaving him soiled.

One day, while I'm watching *Sans Soleil* again, my son comes into my office, watches Marker's film over my shoulder, is mesmerized, and begins to watch it over and over. Soon he is quoting long passages to me while we eat breakfast together. At Christmas, we visit my parents and I tell them about learning of Sal and how my own ignorance seems to keep blooming like a dark cloud. Then I leave for a conference. While I'm gone, my son gets the whole family to look for Sal. It isn't in any of their old atlases. They forget to tell me that they've done this work on my behalf. Later, back home, I hear my son telling the story of their search. I say, "I don't remember that." He says, "Of course you don't. You weren't there." Of course you don't, you weren't there. And in Cape Verde? Even if we were there, we weren't really there. There. Moving spots in time, geography, action, engagement, and relation.

Today, I tell my son that I'm trying to finish writing up this story and how confused I am. He says, "Oh I just found Ile de Sal on Google Earth. Want to see it?"

We start with a view of the planet from the stars, swoop in, dizzyingly, burst down through the clouds, Africa flies up at us, the ocean spreading out like spilled ink. Quickly. Falling. Vertigo. Then we are swooping toward a few islands, a brown blotch appears and grows. Then stops. Sal. A barren desert island. The pixilated ocean, squares of blue and green collaged against its beige shore. Some clouds. It looks empty. My son says, "Try zooming in more. You always need to zoom in more." We click an arrow and start to lower onto, then into, a cluster of puffy clouds. And there, suddenly, is a building, Cape Verde's Amilcar Cabral International Airport. Next to it, on the runway, the shapes of three planes. Briefly, both past and present come into focus. Briefly, I sense the convergence of family and history, see my mother, feel her squeeze my hand, and let go.

the necessity to explore form a bore. Namibia's not a border, nor a country, but a cloud from 1915 forward, territory's contest goes under in some stories and some lives, both from above and below.[3] Some days the farm is just a farm, some days an outpost, or a Bantustan, some days it's making someone's fortune, for my cousin, he was fighting on the border meant Angola. Namibia there, not there. Angola a light to die for. He saw action, a fraction, that divides, then what acronym remembers the other coast's renamo v. frelimo, a double dutch vision of the finger in two dikes an opening for a joke in my world view from a satellite tracking you as you smoke in the back yard, relief a beeping star tracking yr beautiful assassin dreams my love, zoom in.

O angel-wreckage, turn around, there's only a blank page where Ricoeur's exalted and humiliated subjects may embrace. "Someday"'s a lash. Futurity gets you through the day only to end it. "Indefinite detention" is today's special latex helix. Even the most promising nascent nations seem shackled by habitual structures. What is it that is longed for after liberation? When, as Cabral said, "the real work begins"? Some other way of being. But in a world of nations, there's small space for alternatives, though we barely know what a nation is.[4] Ask again: What is born at the birth of a nation? Who can tell this story?

Freedom Day

I.

"[T]he telling of the individual story and the individual experience," Fredric Jameson writes, "cannot but ultimately involve the whole laborious telling of the collectivity itself."[8] The whole laborious telling of the collectivity. And of the individual. And their inseparability. The self, the family, the society; their tensions and dissolutions. The interwoven narratives, the absence of narratives, the facts, their fleeing.

The self, the family, the society; their tensions and dissolutions. Margaret Thatcher said, "There is no such thing as society. There are individual men and women, and there are families."[9] Her brutal erasure of non-familial associations of individuals, of the collectivity, is, perversely, at once a malevolent mistake and an ideological truth. The lens of personal relations, of family, inevitably shapes the way we see, and act in, society. But that doesn't mean there is no such thing as society.

So often, I want to erase in competition with Thatcher, out at the other end of the spectrum, the autobiographical end where families and individuals only seem to be what is known (what "there is" for Thatcher). I want to wipe out that narrow view and focus only on the larger picture. To say, There are only societies. And yet, it is so hard to escape the family as entry point, the way both structural understandings of the familial and our own personal experience of family inform our social and political relations.

These are questions of blood. The blood myth of family. The blood of political struggles. The crossings of place, politics, the personal. The desire to leave them behind. Their pull. Their possibilities.

— 32 —

Is it ever possible to choose our families or our nations? Or our race? Where and how can we make this real? And what does it mean for us that our national identities are so often formed as early and as intimately as the rest of our sense of self? For those born into families of privilege and power, or even into the bosom of the oppressor, what conditions make it possible for them to renounce those privileges? For those who are born into oppression, what enables resistance? For those who want to act, but fear, what conditions might offer courage, support, hope?

In his book *The Principle of Hope* (written in the 1930s while in exile from Nazi Germany), the philosopher Ernst Bloch wrote that the way into a utopian future demands a "dreaming forward" that relies on an understanding of both present and past. For Bloch, "world history itself is an experiment—a real experiment conducted in the world and aimed towards a possible just and proper world." The example of South Africa seems, at first, to fit so nicely here; the pariah nation transformed into a symbol of possibility. Nelson Mandela smiling and waving as he walks out of prison and into the presidency. Of course, the recent history of South Africa is not so neat, nor is its present.

We are accustomed to turning to history for answers and guidance. But precisely how is understanding history a crucial part of creating our present and future? Or, is Walter Benn Michaels right to claim that "history makes us who we are, but it's also, for the purpose of making our society more just—at least if we identify justice with equal opportunity—irrelevant." Michaels is interested in offering a critique of the rise of identity politics, in which he sees a problematic movement "to replace the differences betweens what people think (ideology) and the differences between what people own (class) with the differences between what people are (identity)." As part of his critique, Michaels reminds us that while identity politics has an interest in "the history that makes us who we are," this "interest in the past shouldn't be mistaken for an analysis of or an attempt to deal with the problems of the present. It's one thing to celebrate Black History Month; it's another thing to redistribute wealth."[10]

2.

"Ten years of democracy!" the newspapers at home celebrated. This seemed like the time to return.

There is a cousin who will drive to the celebrations. The city is quiet. Empty. The city is closed for the holiday. The newspaper here tells us that celebrations have been cancelled for lack of money. There are no celebrations. There is a white family on a blanket in the park. The father says, "Ten years of what, eh kids?" "Democracy" they answer flatly without looking up from whatever they are playing. Other people, non-white people ("now we say 'previously disadvantaged communities'") say, "There might be something happening at the stadium." We chat. People talk about access to jobs, voting, rights. People speak of poverty, the gap between poor and rich, the lack of housing, overcrowded schools, AIDS, violence, crime. People say this. People say that. Many of them simply shrug about ten years of democracy. Ten years seems like a much longer time here than at home.

I have flown from a place, a time, and a position where apartheid still seemed to be the defining aspect of South Africa to a place, a time, and a multitude of positions where that is more complicated. Here, it feels like the Fourth of July. Staged, empty, meaningless. Here, freedom is old news, is history; poverty and crime are present. It's one thing to celebrate Freedom Day; it's another to redistribute wealth.

Time, distance, change and its absence all seem to be hovering around a moment when the present turns into the past. Maybe the awareness of history's emergence is part of what defines any time of vivid transition. Maybe, post-revolution, there is also always a sense of history slipping away, of history becoming "irrelevant."

3.

Today, with the people in the park, a resigned "whatever" reigns. But next year on this day, "UnFreedom Day" will be celebrated, or rather "mourned" or "decelebrated," for the first time by the shackdweller movement, Abahlali baseMjondolo, which calls itself "the largest organisation of the militant poor in post-apartheid South Africa" and which protests against the national holiday when "Once again the poor will be herded into stadiums so that the politicians can tell the people to celebrate their freedom."[11] As Breyten Breytenbach, in *The Memory of Birds in the Time of Revolution,* puts it, "Only the poor can break the cycle of exploitation and dependence. Power makes stupid." Breytenbach continues:

> Neither religion nor ideology nor even art will permit the dominators to understand the underdogs. Utopian collectivism, just like free trade capitalism, is a European export notion nurtured on Northern greed and uncertainty and dogmatic dreams.... It is only by generating and mobilizing Africa's capacity to think from its own reality, to transform its conditions so as to live within its means, that the grip of European charity and paternalism and cultural cannibalism (and the pleasure Westerners get from feeling guilty), so corrosive to Africa's self-image, can be loosened.[5]

But today, I'm searching for some "Utopian collectivism." Where would "we" be without it? Is this "we" really impossible? I can't accept that. I think of Martin Luther King saying, "I refuse to accept despair as the only response to the ambiguities of history."

Today, the road blockade that will lead to the emergence of the shack-dweller movement is a year in the future. Today, the paper here says there will be a big celebration in Pretoria, the capitol, a celebration that will be broadcast to large screens in stadiums throughout the country. Apparently there is no screen in central Cape Town. My cousin and I start to drive out to one of the townships to find a screen, but we are thwarted by roadblocks. We detour. More roadblocks. We give up, and decide to visit a family reunion campsite, telling ourselves that we don't really want to watch television today.

Tomorrow, the television will show the first pictures from Abu Ghraib. There will be reports of "misconduct" and of torture. Tomorrow, everyone will watch television.

Tomorrow, we will begin again the whole laborious telling of the collectivity. And of the individual. And their inseparability. The self, the family, the society; their tensions and dissolutions. The interwoven narratives, the absence of narratives, the facts, their fleeing.

small bees crawl from the ground by the handful. Dusty brown not gold. Anxiety ticks its way. Processes don't unfold, but whir. Days panic, and stack up. There are no calamities, only more bees. Equilibrium's dishwater, turpentine. Turpentine's dishwater, a serpent. Road blocks are permanent, despite the flagmen.

?

↳ no order

Robben Island

It is early. Dark, but the mountains still darker. I can just see the long scarf of woolly gray mist on the river. By the side of the road, three people squat next to a little fire, orange against the black. Another cluster a mile down the road and then another. Wool caps and bare legs. I warm my hands on the car heater's vent. I offer no rides. I am alone. I feel justified. I try to hide. I turn up the music. It is gorgeous. Everything outside is obscenely gorgeous. I try not to blame the music. I can critique the aestheticizing urge, but I can't resist it. Driving in Africa, a constant oscillation: ecstasy, shame, ecstasy, shame.

The light rises like a tide, imperceptible. Vineyards emerge, graphs of gnarled black vines crisscrossing the hills. I make this part of the drive every day. I notice that I feel proprietary about it. *My* stretch of road. *My* pleasure. But today I'll go farther than my children's school, all the way to Cape Town where I'll catch a boat to Robben Island, site of the prison that, for decades, held Mandela and other South African revolutionaries. The sun crests into my rearview mirror halfway to the city. I drive blind for several minutes, washed in white, missing night's black. Ahead, a long tongue of smog maps my route.

I stop at my cousin's house in the city for a cup of tea before heading down to the ferry to the prison. We sit on the patio and watch Table Mountain turn from blue to slate gray. I'm in reporter mode, checking my cassette recorder, putting a notebook in my pocket, pretending to have some real reason to be here while, truly, I'm not sure what that reason is. I say that I'm using my privileged access to travel in order to understand something about political violence that might help me disrupt it in my own world. But maybe I'm simply trying to reconnect with my lost family. Or maybe it's the need to navigate these poles of the personal and the political that brings me here.

Today, because I'm going to tour the past, the talk turns away from where to get the best rusks (Woolworths) to the released political prisoners—formerly termed "terrorists"—who now lead the tours on Robben Island. My cousin says that as white children in South Africa, they learned there was "a terrorist in every tree." I tell her that my children are learning "either you are with us or you are with the terrorists."[13] Our talk turns from terrorism to war. My cousin holds her mug with both hands, warming them, pulls her knees up to her chest, props her feet on the wrought iron table and says *I had a friend who fought in Zimbabwe. He said they'd cut off victim's fingers and string them into necklaces.*

She frowns and sips her tea. She says, *I heard your soldiers in Iraq made their prisoners eat pork, made them drink from toilets.* I say nothing. I think, *my* soldiers. I drink my tea. She says, *I blame war, the institution.* Blame. I think, I blame myself. But I like her answer better. Let's send war to jail. And national identity, too.

The boat ride only adds to my nausea. Huge inky swells lifting and dropping away. The kelp beds far below swaying thickly. I've seen them replicated in enormous tanks at the aquarium back in town. Brown, amber, green. Rubbery underwater ribbons rising like smoke, dipping like kites coming down. The boat groans loudly on.

The island is barren. The light in the prison yard is an implement, it screeches, is something to be avoided. I'm on the tour with S. He tells the crowd of tourists, some white, some black, mostly from Europe and England, that he was arrested for activities committed as part of his work with MK, Umkhonto We Sizwe, "the spear of the nation," the armed wing of the ANC. That he was arrested as a "terrorist." S. tells his story several times a week. I've been on his tour before. Sometimes he leaves out whole chapters.

As we drive past a small house, S. tells how Robert Sobukwe, the first President of the Pan Africanist Congress (PAC), was kept in isolation there. When Sobukwe was arrested for his anti-apartheid political activities in 1960, Parliament enacted a "General Law Amendment Act" that gave the Minister of Justice the power of indefinite detention for political prisoners. This became known as the "Sobukwe Clause" as it was used year after year to keep him locked up. After nine years in prison, Sobukwe was finally released, but was kept under house arrest until his death in 1978.

Sobukwe argued that black South Africans needed to "liberate themselves" without the help of non-blacks. A precursor to Biko and the Black Consciousness movement, Sobukwe was vigorously opposed to white liberal arguments in favor of "multi-racial" anti-apartheid approaches. In 1959, he said:

> To us the term "multi-racialism" implies that there are such basic insuperable differences between the various national groups here that the best course is to keep them permanently distinctive in a kind of democratic apartheid. That to us is racialism multiplied, which probably is what the term truly connotes. We aim, politically, at government of the Africans by the Africans, for the Africans, with everybody who owes his only loyalty to Africa and who is prepared to accept the democratic rule of an African majority being regarded as an African. We guarantee no minority rights, because we think in terms of individuals, not groups.

Sobukwe's compelling vision promoted a "non-racialism" focused both on ending white domination and on making all individuals responsible as Africans—as members of a United States of Africa.

The bus drives on, past an outlying building, a community hall of sorts. On my first trip to Robben Island, I came with a cousin. As we passed this building he said, "This is where we had our dances. As university students. It was a novelty. The wardens had a band. The prison cooks catered the food. We were waited on by prisoners. The students would get drunk and stand on the bow of the boat on the way home and get their tuxedos soaked with spray." Seasickness. Nausea.

Another cousin once told me about someone she knew whose father was a guard at Robben Island who said they would have William Tell night with tins cups on the heads of the prisoners. She doesn't say what they used as ammunition. She adds that they threw mud pies at Mandela, and that when this guard met Mandela after freedom, Mandela said, "that is the past; we must move forward." I mention these stories to our guide, S., and ask how hard it is to simply "move forward" from this past. He says, "It took a hundred years to gain liberation. It will take another hundred to gain equality."

The bus passes the lime quarry where the prisoners worked and sometimes led a course of prison studies that helped keep the movement alive. We park back at the central buildings and S. gives the tourists some time to explore the yard where Mandela, Sisulu and the others chipped rock and sewed clothes. We all peer at faded photographs of these men mounted under glass. Later, we will buy reproductions of these photos. I will buy my children a stuffed Nelson Mandela doll.

S. sits with me on a bench in the shade. We talk about television. Did I see the Brenda Fassie special? Yes. Brenda Fassie, pop star, wild woman, "Madonna of the Townships" died a few weeks ago after a long struggle with drug addiction. Did I see Reagan's funeral? No. He shakes his head, says, *Your people love him. He's a hero now.* I shake my head. No. He must be wrong.

I look down at the bright red Coke can I'm drinking from. It is printed with a special collectors' edition message. "Milestones of Democracy." I get Milestone #8. "First South African in Space." The caption reads, "Our democracy has become our passport to endless possibilities. In 2002 Mark Shuttleworth became the first South African to embark on a 10-day space safari." Space safari. The astronaut floats weightless and helmeted on the shiny red can, a black visor hiding his white face. Maybe he's waving down at us. Or winking. Wanted: Benjamin's "dialectical optic" that "perceives the everyday as impenetrable, the impenetrable as everyday."[14]

Hey, S. breaks in, suddenly animated. He asks if I saw this week's edition of South Africa's version of "Lifestyles of the Rich and Famous." Yes, I saw it. I saw it because one of my cousin's houses was featured. I cringe. He can't know this. He says, Jesus. *That house, the farm. Sexwale, man, the fucker.* I sigh. He's seen a different segment, a different house. Tokyo Sexwale, former member of Biko's Black Consciousness Movement, former MK member, former Marxist, former Robben Island political prisoner—his pallet, his shit bucket, just down the row—has become a leading businessman, the Donald Trump of South Africa (he even hosted the South African version of *The Apprentice*) who now lives in a gracious mansion. We should be glad, right? I wait for S. to speak. He says, *The man is worth five hundred million dollars. The richest black man in the nation.*

Something about the word "nation" catches me. I ask, *You ever read Frantz Fanon?* S. whips his head around, looks at me through his dark glasses and leaps to his feet. *Frantz Fanon! Frantz Fanon! Fanon was right! Pitfalls of national consciousness, man! Base the revolution on the nation and when you win, the terms of nation win with you. Ach, man, the guy is rolling in his grave, or laughing. Look around. Look around.*

Later that afternoon, in the library, I read Fanon on the "Pitfalls of National Consciousness." He wrote:

> Before independence, the leader generally embodies the aspirations of the people for independence, political liberty, and national dignity, but as soon as independence is declared, far from embodying in concrete form the needs of the people in what touches bread, land, and the restoration of the country to the sacred hands of the people, the leader will reveal his inner purpose: to become the general president of that company of profiteers impatient for their returns which constitutes the national bourgeoisie.[6]

S. shakes his head. *You been to Khayalitsha? That's where I live. You think Sexwale comes around? Huh. He's kissed that all goodbye.* I hesitate, then ask, *So Sexwale sold out?*

S., sounding both angry and wistful, says, *You saw the house, right? And the animals?* He sighs. *Beautiful animals.* He turns, gestures for me to follow him to our next stop, Nelson Mandela's cell, and steps out of the shade and into the bright prison yard full of waiting tourists.

in minerals. What's not to say? ~~Saying is everything.~~ Without saying, drift, solecism, defeat. Don't not say anything. Don't say any- thing. Don't not stop those double negatives. My tattoo says: weather or not, history is taking our time

Arboretum (Stinkwood, fever tree, sweet thorn, palm)

> What kind of times are they, when
> A talk about trees is almost a crime
> Because it implies silence about so many horrors?
>
> —Bertolt Brecht, "To Those Born Later"

Morning steams the fog from the river. The subject is more fog than river. A swirl of bedclothes and hairspray lifts off the water just ahead. A long smoky scarf of dawn. We're in an aisle of blue gum trees, impossibly tall, the bark peeling from their trunks like a sunburn. Papery, more pink than blue in this light. Gravestones in the shadows among the trees. Three black men stand around a small fire they've made inside a low marble wall next to a funerary angel, green-black mold covering its wings.

Desecration, my aunt murmurs, her thighs shushing in their snug, soft lavender pants. A wave of litter blows past our ankles. An empty plastic bag sticks in a tall clump of grass.

Gouyemora, one tall man with dreadlocks yells at us, not smiling. My aunt grips my hand in her thin bony one. Her gold rings are soft and cool against my palm. We nod and reply, *Gouyemora, gouyemoura. Good morning. Hoe gaan dit?* We smile brightly. The word "cowed" emerges with us from the alley of trees, the dark slash through the cemetery to the river beyond, its fog still rising in a thick cloudy layer. It swirls and moves. Blueish like the smoke rising from the little fire.

Two men squat by the river's edge, wool caps pulled low over their dark faces, one in blue coveralls. They say good morning more gently than the first group. Everyone smiles and nods. What do they see? Two rich white women, women with the leisure time to go for a walk on a week-day morning. Women with clean stretchy clothes that they use just for walking. (Maybe women who should just leave Africa, having had so much of it already. Give it back.)

Family was pretty rich and benefited from apartheid

Later, another aunt says, *I think that if you're not on board with the long difficult process of transition to democracy, actually, you must go live some-where else.* As she says this, flocks of golfers drift past the fountained yard of her gated estate.

Here we are in what Fanon called, "the present of the people's history," the "zone of occult instability where the people dwell."[16]

Here the trail passes the entrance to the arboretum where my aunt sighs and says, *It is so beautiful in there. I used to walk there all the time, mile after mile of trees and plants from all over the world. Asia. America. Africa. A whole world of trees. It is too dangerous now. You can't go in at all. Let's go back.* Back out, leave it to itself, someone's dream of global botanical miscegenation.

It's wild now, she says. *Desperate people live there.* They sleep on card-board under baobabs, or starry ginkos, or flame trees. (*We used to call them kaffir trees, but we're not allowed to now.*) Their home in the arbore-tum is gorgeous beyond words, but cold. Cold in winter, cold at night, cold this morning. We turn back to the road and hustle up the hill past Victorian houses with potted plants on the stoops, graying fountains on the lawns. We move quickly under the lush foliage.

Stinkwood, fever tree, sweet thorn, palm.

in the trees, the melancholy impossibility of being other sinks the bob-
ber. Still, there's a gullet full of others to be loved including
strangers (shown here in the margin of a death certificate by a
smudged fingerprint with the word "sorry!" scrawled next to it).

II. Letters

Dear A,

I am still in South Africa, so far from home, from you. Your idea that we write only on paper was sweet, but I'm done with it. Still no letter or poems from you. They say it can take eight weeks. I've waited four. Meanwhile, my own last letter drifts idly over the water, seasick and irritated by the patch behind its ear. Or maybe my letter has taken a land route through Siberia and over the Bering Straight. It'll arrive tired and bearing little resemblance to its former self.

The journey will seem pointless and my letter will have a hard time focusing, always looking over one shoulder, even more sentimental than when it left me, its nostalgic mother. Finally, it will sit, suffocating and bored in your box for weeks and weeks while you're away, settling, going flat, forgetting even the long journey, which might once have left some trace of adventure, despite the fatigue. You see where this leads? Nowhere. Nowhere. You are nowhere and so am I as long as these plodding little over-valued slips of paper are relied upon. Why the stubborn refusal of e-mail? People used to pay fast riders to get letters to their destinations in haste. I will pay the fast rider. I will pretend that it is not a worldwide anesthetic of false immediacy that I turn to and will send my best blueblack horse, loosed from its traces, riding at night and meeting the cigarette boat I've arranged to have waiting at the bay. And then, my little letter will be zinging and singing, dressed in her tourist beads, sunbathing on the bow. She'll step off with salt on her skin and Cape wine or township beer on her breath and say, come on, come on! Africa is only a puppet-legged giraffe away from wherever you are. My little house in Simondium is only a baboon in the kitchen away from the raccoons in your trash.

Surely you too are drinking something made from grapes? Here I am, knee deep in Sauvignon Blanc and fallen leaves—crumpled, brown-edged, yellow, red. They blow in from the vineyards, scurry around the car in the morning, and scoot across the street in front of the school in the afternoon while I wait for all the boys in their striped blue blazers to move in herds over the zebra crossing. Dozens and dozens of them, those blazers hanging crooked on their thin shoulders, faces glowing, loosening their ties, taking off their shoes, walking barefoot, and shouting in a mix of Afrikaans, English, Xhosa, and Zulu. One smaller boy jogs in and out among their hips, navy school bag jouncing. It is my son, with his grin and his dimple. His new friends wave from where they lean against the bulgy black trunks of the gargantuan oak trees. On the way home, we make a stop to say hello to my mother's nanny in the old-age home next door, where my kids breathe through their mouths to avoid the smell of urine and Lysol and drift out into the hall while I rub Nanny's papery brown arm and ask her to tell me about when she and her family were forced from their home, their neighborhood, to tell me about my mother as a little girl. She says only, "Those were happy, happy times." And I want to believe her. Or, "Ach, so long ago." And really, why should she tell me anything?

Then it's down the long road before dark comes (so early here as winter approaches in the far far south) hoping to avoid the attacks everyone warns me dusk often brings, here where the crime rate is the highest in the world, where the extreme disparity between haves and have-nots makes that violence intelligible. We drive past the brickfields where precarious red mastabas smoke all day, their fireplace smell already a smell of nearly home, past the workers hitching out to our part of town where we all live under tin roofs, but I have concrete walls and they may not, past the bakkies (little trucks) full of farm hands with dark skins jolting past the heavy-shouldered gates of the wineries, past the rusted combis that look like determined potato bugs and drive so slowly they have to straddle the shoulder all the time to let people like us in our little blue Nissan fly past. Past the field full of black and white hook-beaked ibises (laughing "*Hah. Hah. Hah-dee-dah*"), a misplaced scene from Egypt, down our bumpy dirt drive to scare off the peacocks who clong around on our roof, big chickens in silly tiaras, crowing loudly, "*How? Mao? Cow? Wow.*" One, a movement in the window, a crown blown by wind, feathery pistils and stamens, a huge white one sits on the sill, silent, impossible, until a *La Jetée* eyeblink makes it real. In the yard, guinea fowl, black with white speckles, sound like they're riding by with a playing card stuck in their bicycle spokes, like a piece of paper in a fan: *tick-tick-tick-tick, chirr, chirr, whirrrrrr*. And every day, outside my window, doves: *Awe Awe ah ah ah ah*. Quarter note. Quarter note. Rest. Sixteenth, eighth, repeat. *Why don't... you write to me? / Boo hoo... I cry for you.*

Dinner made on a hot plate, bedtime stories of pepperpots and pigtails and then back to my work table, my happy pile of books, CDs of Bach and Brenda Fassie. I think they are kissing cousins, both wanting things light and fast, halogen and helium, striking the match for the firework called the hydraheaded lumen time stopper, then miserable and furious, working until the ink-soaked paper blackens and parts, reminding them of the ruin they had meant to avoid.

Some mornings I lie in the bath thinking of you when I should be frying eggs (*sunnyside, sing sunnyside*), tying ties (*once around, twice around, rabid through the rabbit hole*), and getting down to the charge of culling complicity from colonization. (*Hey you, enemy of my enemy's enemy, wanna see my panga, whack my machete into your baby to stave off future losses.*) I close my eyes again and hear my own child's shuddering pleas outside the bathroom door. Sweet baby buster crying *please don't send me to school. Please, please. I really really really want to be with you.* I say, *Get ready. I'd let you stay, but I don't have much time.* He says, *please, please, I really, really, really want to stay.* Rigid after forty rounds, I really really really want to shake him to a full stop.

Recognition = distance closing like a smack on skin.

Some nights there is a shushing wind in the lofty dark pompoms of the blue gum tree. Someone scratched those stars in the sky so I could show you how stagecraft works. Keep your head tipped back. You'll see something soon. I'm right here, disappearing your pupils. Wait. Come back. There's never to deal with. Still, every day, there's wanting to make this all last and last, at least through next week when I'll go back to Langa, and then to look again at the exhibit at the District Six museum that shows how racial classifications were policed under apartheid. The pencil test in kinky hair, the confusions at the boundaries of race, the children of "white" or "colored" parents who came out "too dark." One pass photo looks just like my mother whose family is "white," but, as she says, "Clearly, there's some black blood in there." She has olive skin and dark hair. (Once, I went to pick up a well-known African American poet at an airport and when we met, some look in my face made her ask, "Did you expect me to look blacker?" and I blurted out, "No, it's just that you look just like my mother. I thought you were my mother." But she asked the right question. My brother is even darker than my mother. When he works in Egypt, he passes for Egyptian. As a child in the U.S., kids would say, "hey black boy." And, then, well, you've seen my pale skin.

Next week, I'll also pore over police transcripts from the 1970s and '80s. What am I looking for? Why would I want to relive that? To understand? To pretend any understanding would change the future? A sick voyeuristic thrill? Still, this too will go into that box labeled Make It Last. Which I have to close late at night when there are distant or nearby shouts and the security alarm goes off and unknown people bang on my door at midnight and yell things I don't understand, but should, and I end up sitting up with a stomachache planning the fastest route home, but then remembering that the airport lies at the end of the Hell Run (fill your tank, lock your doors, and don't slow down for anything) where a woman was stoned last week and killings are not unknown.

Fear has a tailwind. Fear colonizes quickly. Fear is calculating red lights and bystanders and petrol levels even now as I write you this letter upside down under the Southern Cross.

This is the part where I'm flying. Out over the shadows of fields and empty roads. Midnight in the country isn't so very dark once you get high enough. And I am very high. There is milky light everywhere. I whistle your name in Braille, uselessly. I am fanning your letters out, willing them to make a suit. Wishing your love of lonely words and warped syntax would make way for the grammar of love. It is an arrow, not a bunch of feathers. It is a one-lane road, not a clover-leaf. Didn't you read that book? [This is the nature of the differend.]

C

down a line of brown river, an eaglet screams a heron, where your legs (logs) look in the same direction, quiet as your walk, a stutter's a sign of desire. Or not. The birds: the thread that's pulled. Gravel is (our) language. Gravel is (no) language. Wakoski said connecting past to present is what earth is all about. From that history to this eros isn't only apparatus.

Dear A,

I am in the Manuscripts and Archives Division of the University of Cape Town's Special Collections, reading through files documenting the work of a women's anti-apartheid group, the Black Sash, whose rallies my mother attended as a student. I have been here every day for several days. I am not sure what I'm doing. I seem to be enjoying myself. I've had groundnut stew with scholars and students from all over Africa at the African café at the top end of the building and tea and falafel at the kosher café at the bottom of the building. Sometimes I sneak over to the library's Virginia Woolf collection and read bits of *The Waves* ("I am tied down with single words") and think about you. And I have seen stacks of documents, photographs, and newspaper clippings recording the brutalities of apartheid.

There are atrocities in the archives. There are black and white photos of wounds, decapitations, and charred bodies. Why are they here? Why look at them? What can this do? What faith in representation's utility sustains this space? At first, it seems that this is no longer reportage, but history; there's no perpetrator to stop now. But, the pendulum swings to remind us that there are, of course, still perpetrators to stop, and that one of the powers of reportage is to live both in and beyond its moment, to remind us that history, or histories, do not conclude. As Robert Duncan wrote to Charles Olson, "There's no place that the past can take place except right now when we consider it. The past has no other existence." The archives ask how we can still believe that reminders of past horrors might prevent future ones. But maybe what is also being preserved in the archive is naiveté. Naiveté as hope. Optimism instead of pessimism. The possibility that every researcher sorting through the archive of oppression might opt to stop writing and start working in her own world.

Each time I open a new box describing the horrors of the past, I have thought of leaving them behind. I have thought of Shoshana Felman telling us that "testimony cannot be simply relayed, repeated or reported by another without thereby losing its function as testimony."[17] I have thought of her praise of Celan as one whose disruption of "conscious meaning" allows his words to "enact" rather than merely report. I have thought of Celan; I have tried not think of Celan. I have thought of Claude Lanzmann saying that his film *Shoah* was not meant "to transmit knowledge" and that to try to "learn the Holocaust" is, in fact, to "forget" it.[18] Is this also true for apartheid?

Surely there is a place for testimony beyond its initial telling, its initial transcription? Maybe now, with so much more wreckage piled behind us, events might be able to be "intelligible" and also maintain what Felman calls the "unassimilable shock of history."[19] I'm hesitant to give up completely on the value of reportage's legacy, to say that it is inevitably ineffectual.

Michel de Certeau spoke of writing that aims to "understand" and thus hides alterity, "calming the dead who still haunt the present," and "offering them scriptural tombs." He wrote that "the dear departed find a haven in the text *because* they can neither speak nor do harm anymore. These ghosts find access through *writing* on the condition that they remain *forever silent*." But is it impossible to listen to the dead? Surely the testimony of certain individuals or the description of certain events can't just be left behind, can't, when they shock us, just be ignored and placed, with white gloves, carefully back in their acid-free tombs.

From The Black Sash Advice Office Collection
University of Cape Town Archives [7]

* Memo: August 19, 1976. Heading: Township Distur-
bances. Victim: ████████. Summary: Killing. Notes:
People around were throwing stones at the riot squad.
People started running. ████████ was sitting with
friends watching the rioting when he was shot in the
left shoulder. He was taken to Gugulethu Police station by the riot squad but died of his wound. His
mother, Mrs. B., found out when returning home from
work. His family found him at the Salt River Mortuary.

* Victim: Mrs. ████████████████. Her son
went missing on Wednesday night. She went to Tygerberg
Hospital, the Gugulethu Police, and the Langa Police
Station. He had been shot by the riot squad on the 11th
of August 1976. On the 17th of August his brother found
him at the Salt River Mortuary.

Turn the page in the folder.

* Abduction and killing: ████████████ aged
22. Disappeared 6 pm 11/8/76 when he went out to see
what was happening down the road. Lived at NY84 no
27 Gugulethu with mother and 7 brothers and sisters.
Later that evening she heard he had been shot and had
been taken to (illegible) ward at Tygerberg Hospital.
She called at the hospital 4 times and was told there
was no record of his being (illegible) there. She then
called at Salt River mortuary on 13/8/76 and 19/8/76

but was told he wasn't there. On 6/10/76 she was told by police that her son was at Salt River mortuary where he had been since 12/8/76. She was told he had been shot in the forehead on 11/8/76, taken to Tygerberg Hospital where a doctor certified him as dead at 12:05 AM on 12/8/76. His Reference Book was in his jacket pocket. He was buried on 9/10/76. Copy of letter for his mother and Burial Cert. attached.

* Mrs. ██████████████: The police beat Mrs. ████████ with batons and pushed her into a van and took her to Gugulethu Police Station where she was detained. She is the mother of 7 children and works as a domestic in Mowbray.

Turn the page in the folder.

* Killing: ██████ was shot dead on NY 115 on the way home from school on 14 September, 1976.

* Reports of severe ill treatment: smashed elbow, pellet wound, shot and thus crippled and mentally disabled, shot through hips by riot police, shot in the throat.

There are dozens of folders. Two hours later, I am reading the reports from 1985. There are so many. Bullets separate them.

• ████████████ was preparing for work at home in the early morning when a policeman kicked open the door and shot him in the knee from the doorway. The policeman then went next door and shot at some of the neighbors. A black policeman arrived and called the white policeman to witness his deed. The white replied, "Let me just finish him off."

- Victim: Shot in the face after tear-gassing by police while waiting at the water tap. "I felt a teargas smoke and felt a bullet shot on my left side of my face. I fell to the ground. I was unconscious and I woke up on Tuesday the 19th (the next day). I was unable to speak. I was under police guard day and night. The police did not take any statements from me. I was not taken to the police station."

- Report: ▓▓▓▓▓▓▓▓▓ was walking down street and stopped to cross Terminus when he was shot from a passing police van. Had multiple wounds to body and face.

- ▓▓▓▓▓▓▓▓▓ was shot while walking home by police. He had extensive wounds in stomach, chest, and hands.

- Severe ill treatment: The one-month old baby grandchild of ▓▓▓▓▓▓▓ was tear gassed inside her home and had to be hospitalized with serious breathing and swallowing problems.

- ▓▓▓▓▓▓ was shot while running away from police, wounded in back and arm. He still cannot use his right arm properly.

- Summary: the family were attacked in their house by witdoche wielding pangas. The son was taken to a nearby field and severely assaulted with a knob-kierie. [19 pages of narrative are attached here.]

- Assault with knife, axes, and stones by Cosmo's Football Club hostel dwellers. Police in collusion with attackers.

- Assault on UDF member (axe attack) by members of Azanyu. Mr. ████████ was beaten on his back with axes.

- Severe assault and torture, assault interrupted by arrival of Black Sash women.

- The three black plain-clothes policemen chased me and when I fell, one of them pointed a gun at me. They picked me up and started to hit me with a sjam-bok and their hands. They kicked me and told me to get in the van. They beat me at the police station and asked about the burning of someone's house. I said I didn't know. I didn't know.

- ███████████████. His house was burnt 26 Dec. & his wife killed. He was away at the time.

- ██████████. 2 children born here in Cape Town, 16 yrs boy, 13 yrs girl. Comments: Both her children were taken by the Security Police on the 21st of September in the early hours of the morning, now she doesn't know their whereabouts.

- Beatings with broomsticks—on the face and neck until the broomstick broke, and with quirts and more sjamboks.

- Abducted and raped by soldiers while walking alone to a relatives house. "The two soldiers they were rough. I bled."

- ████████████████████. Mrs ██████ states that on 26/12/76 at about 2 pm she went to look for her two daughters who had gone visiting friends -- she was worried because of the troubles... when she came back in a few minutes she saw that the fighting had started -- her husband was killed and the house burnt down. She was also shot.

- Newspaper clipping: The Cape Times November 17, 1976. Headline: "Police Give Riot toll: 97 killed and at least 417 injured. The subhead reads: "No Whites."

I stop taking notes. On the way home, I stop at the aquarium with its darkened rooms of quiet underwater life—hoping to clear my head. Maybe Claude Lanzmann was right that to learn horror is to forget it.

in the archives, boxed documents. Acid-free or not. In the aquarium, box jellyfish pulse up the darkened tank. The sign says they'll kill a man in three minutes. Spineless anemone, unfurl the tendril. Predatory, rudimentary, medusa, paralysis. (Behind the touch pool's watery arc, the smiling docent says, "on your hand, only a prick.") Catalogue the earlobe on the page: Pinna, crura, scapha, concha, intertragic notch. Close my eyes and. Paper, tissue, ash. Come for me at closing. Cover me with clippings.

Dear A,

Today, the students at the University of Cape Town protested. A few dozen stood at the bottom of the long, wide steps up Table Mountain to neoclassical, multi-columned Jameson Hall, and there they spray-painted signs until everyone was dizzy on aerosol. Their signs said "Betrayal" and "Say No." Most of the students were black, a few were white. Many wore crimson jump suits with the tops rolled down and tied around their waists, revealing ANC t-shirts. One young man had a cherry red plastic mini-megaphone. In a distorted, staticky voice, he asked passersby, "Are you joining us? Are you joiiiiniiinnngg us?"

The crowd grew steadily. Several dozen milled around the protest area and as many as a hundred watched from picnic tables, low walls, and the wide steps. I took out my notebook, ready to play journalist at this emerging event. A tall young man near me hoisted a banner that said "UCT=Taliban."

The group of placard-bearers began to dance and march and walk and bounce in a rough circle, waving their signs and singing. An old protest song. I asked a girl standing near me what the protest was about and she said, "They want to shorten the study week and exam period. They want us to take two exams a day. It is crazy." I asked if it was strange to hear this song now, to have a protest like this, for this issue; she laughed and said, "No. It is not strange. This is South Africa." The protesters were laughing and eager, they smiled and sang joyously; the spectators smiled and chatted with each other.

I asked a young black man in a Puma tracksuit, "What do you think?"

"Ah, yeah, he began to answer, but was distracted by something. He glanced down to the cell phone in his hand and murmured, "Oh, one missed call" and wandered off.

The students gathered the spectators up in a huge parade and marched down to the bright green rugby field in the late-afternoon sun.

In *The White Album*, Joan Didion wrote of going to a student takeover at San Francisco State, a takeover that came late, was oddly genial, a wannabe protest that felt like an "amiable evasion of routine." Didion wrote of her sense of disorientation on that day as being linked to a phrase that was haunting her then, a line from Pound: "Petals on a wet black bough." She wondered if the line might represent "the aimlessness of the bourgeoisie" and thought about how the "illusion of aim" might be gained from a moment of revolution that seemed, to her, a mere performance of "pragmatic optimisim."

In Soweto in 1976, when the students protested, Reuters reported more than 500 people killed, and estimated that the wounded exceeded 1,000 men, women, and children. Now, I find I am tempted to judge, to feel disorientation, even despair, when these students tell me how little they know of their country's history. "That's in the past," they say.

I can't help but think of Benjamin's "Theses on History," where he asserts that the central threat to history is that of becoming a tool of the ruling class. Is that what is happening here? Here at one of the most elite universities in the country, where these students are poised to become the newest members of the ruling class? Benjamin writes, "Only the historian will have the gift of fanning the spark of hope in the past who is firmly convinced that even the dead will not be safe from the enemy if he wins. And this enemy has not ceased to be victorious." I do not pretend to be that historian, but I seek her and long, impossibly, to protect the dead of earlier protests.

And yet, am I truly mourning the loss of something important? While the intensity of the past struggles does seem diminished and the way it gets overwritten feels like a loss, I have to remind myself that the students' issues are real; their issues are their issues.

Michel de Certeau acknowledged that "[h]istoriography takes for granted the fact that it has become impossible to believe in this presence of the dead that has organized (or organizes) the experience of entire civilizations; and the fact too that it is nonetheless impossible "to get over it," to accept the loss of a living solidarity with what is gone." And Homi Bhaba wrote that "[t]he present of the people's history is a practice that destroys the constant principles of a national culture that attempts to hark back to a 'true' national past, often represented in the reified forms of realism and stereotype." I am reminded that even a revolutionary history, even a recent one, can quickly become a dead story.

Still, interpreting this scene needn't rely on an either/or divide. Surely we can both sympathize with the students' present concerns and lament their loss of certain stories of the past, specific accounts of events that are, in fact, still unfolding. Finally, there is the temptation to turn away, to say, "that's their business—I can't possibly understand it—it is not my place to criticize." This is the lure, but in its respect for the players, it plays to the rulers.

So, what words haunt here? Maybe Duncan's to Olson, again. Or Wallace Stevens: "If the day writhes, it is not with revelations." But really, I am straining here, using this deliberate construction to hide the word that really haunts me, the word that is harder to explain. The word that is also sticky and clings to all the messy bits of loss, longing, and impossibility. The word that really catches me over and over is your name.

to dialogue with the past, not just derive from it,[8] to learn a language that frees association, to Xhosa click the lock on idées fixes, lovely conundrums of intentional oxymorons to work some negative dialectic magic. Poof, you're gone, and terror, oppression are part of the past.

Dear A,

Dreams of you in the snow. Thick and beautiful. You are always walking through it. Dark against the white. You look so dear, treading carefully under the trees where the ice is rippled, I have to look away.

Snow in South Africa is strange. An event. There is a photograph that almost everyone in my family has a print of somewhere in their house. It shows a rare snowfall and is dated 1914. In it, a group of grinning men stand around a snowman they have made. The other day, my cousin pointed out that it wasn't a snowman but a snow woman. He showed me the place where the photo had clearly been retouched. "The boobs" he said, and pointed to where the little stone nipples they'd pushed into her breasts had been whited out. Later, we looked at it again with another cousin. "The bush," he said and pointed out the clump of twigs that had been erased from her crotch. The photo looks different now. Less about the snow and more about the men.

My mom once told me how her uncle drove up one day to say there was snow in the mountains. He piled all the kids in the back of the truck and gave them brandy to keep warm. When they got to the mountains, he stood on the back of the truck and tipped back into the snow. Laughing.

A little while ago, one of my cousins here was showing me some old photos when I saw one of snow in the mountains. There in the foreground are the distinctive long pigtails of my mom's best friend. Big bows. And behind her is, unmistakably, my mother. She looks maybe twelve or thirteen. Slim, in a sweater with her pants tucked into knee-high socks. A few photos further on, there is a man looking down into an old fashioned camera pointed right at us. A picture of one person taking a picture of another. A mirror. A joke. A way for the one doing the representing to see him or herself. Looking at the photo, my cousin says "That's my father." The next picture is of the same man lying in the snow with his hands flying into the air over his head. Laughing. One side of the picture is bleached blank as if it is the first shot in the roll of film. It is clearly the image from my mother's story. I wonder if she remembers this moment, or if she remembers this photo.

The next photo is as black as the last one was white. A picture of the inside of a tiny, dark, sooty room. Kerosene blackened and filled with maybe seven or eight black faces clustered close together. They are posing. But they are not smiling. Some of the men wear battered fedoras. Several children squeeze in the middle, and, down front, is a man I swear I know. His nappy hair sticks up three inches. His broad face and the light in his eyes are intimately familiar. But I can't place him and neither can anyone who sees the photo. He is right here. Vibrant. Present. Gone.

I keep these pictures. My mother, her family in the white drifts of snow, the photographer photographing the photographer, the snow angel uncle, the workers in the dark little room. All Africans. I'll show them to you when I get back.

I have no photos of you. It doesn't matter. I can feel your head in my hands. I can see you standing in the doorway. Looking at me looking at you. Hearing the click of systems. Watching. Waiting.

C

lyric documentary leaves (the gutter's structural gap) assembled shots of unexpected snow or drifts of tents make a stab where metony-my and song won't undermine the record of the real, still there always lies the strap-on seduction of the garish words.

Dear A,

Every morning I lie in the bath in the dark before dawn and murmur your name. At night, I walk to the old hotel bar and buy units of electricity for our cinderblock "cottage." The children say, "It's so cold. It's so cold. How can Africa be so cold?" This week, I wrote you an essay that can't seem to come together. I wrote another, more unified, version, but it felt like all that integration was a lie. So, here's a piece that perversely insists on keeping worlds apart. It is called "Duffer's Drift."

III. Duffer's Drift

Now I am quietly waiting for
the catastrophe of my personality
to seem beautiful again,
and interesting, and modern.

—Frank O'Hara, "Mayakovsky"

I make no plea for my own sagacity. I have ques-
tionably poached on academic territory in which I
can claim at best amateur competence. Writing this
book has convinced me, however, that such an inter-
disciplinary attempt is worth the gamble.

—Eric Lott, *Love and Theft*

In the frenzy of utterance the concern with truth.
Hence the interest of a possible deliverance by
means of encounter. But not so fast. First dirty, then
make clean.

—Samuel Beckett, *The Unnamable*

Ventriloquy
is the mother tongue.

—Rae Armentrout, "Attention"

A dance hall drunkenness doesn't allow for insight into race and remembrance any more than kissing an albino Afrikaner behind the scenes while thinking "killer" or "cousin." Afrikaner means enemy, means family. Albino means pigment, its absence, means race, means racism.⁹ If albinism is most visible when you're "black," does it mean race in reverse or its hyper-realization? Would this mean the whitest person is the blackest? All polarities point accusingly at each other, all dichotomies explode flesh into blood.

"The etymology of the word albino is inextricably linked to Africa, to the ethnic gaze of early visitors to the Black continent. The word, which describes the inherited condition of melanin deficiency, traces its origins back to Portugal's colonial interests in Africa. First used in 1777, the word was employed to describe white-spotted West Africans encountered by colonial explorers. According to reports, Portuguese explorers were confounded by the apparent existence of two distinct African races, and as a result distinguished between Negroes and Albinos. Thus, it was from the exotic possibilities of otherness, and the flawed vision of the ethnic gaze, that we derive the word albino."[10]

The man at the bar has pale blue eyes like shark waters, where I am weeping for a poetics of drunkenness, where trouble typing could yield a reeling anesthesia, an anesthetic syntax. A cocooned stumbling away from difficult real-world devices, like bodies. A dizzy, confused hilarity that could edge into clarity, that would party with and be a party to all that is slippery, is misery. A cottony can't-cope kind of writing that could grind and shimmy to a town hall full of white South Africans dancing blindly to their friends' cover band playing "Sweet Home Alabama" and Bob Marley drowned in beer and brandy. Such sticky irony's so easy it's erased by rows of tables tilting cosmically back toward the bar raised by democracy's promise to turn an interregnum into an intermission graced by a coon show.

I am in the middle of writing this essay when I come across the work of South African artist Pieter Hugo and his photographs of albino individuals. His gallery's website states, "Pieter Hugo believes that people project their desires, fears, fantasies and repulsions upon people with albinism.... these images present a challenge. It is the challenge of seeing differently, of relocating the colonising gaze to see something more than simply a blank body onto which we can project our misguided assumptions. This is not an easy task; it requires a seismic shift in consciousness, and a reformation of language. If we are to suspend our voyeuristic urges, we will of necessity have to step beyond the limits of words, in the process disavowing the traditional meaning of words such as blank."[11]

The bar lies off the dance hall. A tight white room. High ceiling and a wield of people lining up for shots, deafening volume of the cover band hurting your ears. At your elbow, a young guy leached of color (white hair, white skin, a ghost's narcosis) buys a drink, and says he knows you. Says he's been to America and found the people unbelievably stupid. Says *you can't talk to them*. Says he finds they/us/you *shallow and boring and arrogant*. Says he's appalled by the *narrow-minded, self-centered aggression* of our President. Also, he has lovely eyes, like sea glass, pale green-blue and never looking away.

Hugo explains how his project began with an earlier series called "Margin." "'Margin' dealt with people living on the peripheries of modern South African society, and included a portrait of an orphaned albino boy who stood next to a birdbath outside his orphanage. 'I kept returning to this picture' says Pieter. 'Something about it captivated me, the role albinism plays in South African society.'"[12]

On my next trip to South Africa, driving into town from the airport, a cousin tells me about his recent divorce and how he would like to pay off his ex with a valuable photograph he has. We walk into his tiny cottage and he says, "That's the photo." It is a deliriously saturated color photograph of an albino boy at a birdbath, taken by Pieter Hugo.

He says, slurs, *you're all alike.* You're all alike. We're all alike. *Americans are doffer-stupid.* Doffer? Duffer? Dopper? Music occludes the air, thick accent, history. It is hard to understand him.

Duffer: An incompetent, dull-witted, awkward or stupid person.

Dopper: In his book, *My Traitor's Heart*, Rian Malan writes, "When rumors of the Enlightenment penetrated their wilderness, the Afrikaners considered them, consulted their bibles and preachers, and finally reached a consensus: These ideas presented a threat to their survival, and should be suppressed—not only in the world at large, but in their own hearts. Soon, many Afrikaners were calling themselves Doppers, after the little metal caps with which they snuffed out candles. They called themselves Doppers because they were deliberately and consciously extinguishing the light of the Enlightenment, so that they could do what they had to do in the darkness. There are many truths about Afrikaners, but none so powerful and reverberant as this willful self-blinding. It was the central act in our history."[13]

Do what you have to do in the darkness. It is late. Objects start to strobe. Lights leave trails like tracers. If remembrance lies in smashed refractions, we can only build on deformation's high; the prisms just before the blackout swerve to memory's harbors. There is speech, but let's not get excited, since the pronouns and the culture prevent much beyond the girlish. Still, he looks as if he's spoken, some expectant looking forward, backward. I nod, don't say you can't understand. A glass is raised like a bright flag and we drink nothing I have ever tasted. Anesthesia clinks her privilege. Laughter's absence flashes as Afrikaner accents sing the stolen song Mbube[14] and then, *buffalo soldier, win the war for America, if you know your history, then you know where you're coming from, then you wouldn't have to ask me, who the heck do I think I am,   I mean it when I analyze the stench, to me it all makes sense, woy, yoy yoy, woy yoy-yoy yoy.*   Someone's doubled over. People dance, another cover. His look pulls it over and silences the space. He stands, takes my hand, walks to the edge of the floor.

Shortly after the Boer War, a British Major General named Sir Earnest Swinton, using the pseudonym Lieutenant Backsight Forethought, or BF, wrote *The Defence of Duffer's Drift.* (Sir Swinton also revolutionized warfare by his invention of the tank during WWI.) *Duffer's Drift* is considered a military classic on minor tactics and is still used today.

It is structured as a string of dreams:

"Upon an evening after a long and tiring trek, I arrived at Dreamdorp. The local atmosphere, combined with a heavy meal, is responsible for the following nightmare, consisting of a series of dreams. To make the sequence of the whole intelligible, it is necessary to explain that though the scene of each vision was the same, by some curious mental process I had no recollection of the place whatsoever. In each dream the locality was totally new to me, and I had an entirely fresh detachment. Thus, I had not the great advantage of working over familiar ground."

The local atmosphere, combined with a heavy meal, is responsible for the following nightmare. Albino-boy plunges through the throbbing, shoves it out with one hand, hangs on with the other. An arm whips straight until the shoulder cracks its limit socket yanks it back into some slamming chest or book can't tell if he looks knowing, angry, tired, sad, or drunk. Not dancing. Only standing. Sounds of pulsing blood turn ears to liars. Others dance to close the gap. A space mirages clearly there he shoots the body out then reels it back. Under his arm, my breasts are crushed and then uncovered are the ways that more than history keeps us apart and draws us close.

There are maps:

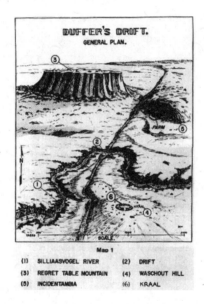

Map 1

(1)	SILLIAASVOGEL RIVER	(2)	DRIFT
(3)	REGRET TABLE MOUNTAIN	(4)	WASCHOUT HILL
(5)	INCIDENTAMBIA	(6)	KRAAL

And lists of lessons:

"To test the concealment or otherwise of your position, look at it from the enemy's point of view."

"Probable cost—some heavy and glib lying."

Some heavy and glib lying. Some desires are not perverse but backward in the alley behind the kitchen tight against the whitewash, a motion is mirrored, mimicked. You are not here. Think don't fuck him. Back-sight. Forethought. We are thrust up against the wall playing our parts. There's both foreground and background, so adjust your eyes. Repellent Afrikaner, enemy of apartheid years, a sign of fascism circa 1976 to me and maybe I to him, circa Monday's empire. Rulers, oppressors, kin, and blood. There's a dizzy oblivion. From "sheer horror" to "libidinal gratification" and back again.[15]

Swinton warns:

"Beware of being taken in reverse."

"Beware of being enfiladed.... You can sometimes avoid being enfiladed by so placing your trench that no one can get into prolongation of it to fire down it, or you can 'wiggle' it about in many ways, so that it is not straight, or make 'traverses' across it."

"Do not have your trench near rising ground over which you cannot see, and which you cannot hold."

"Do not, if avoidable, be in tents when bullets are ripping through them; at such times a hole in the ground is worth many tents."

Do not, if avoidable, be in tents when bullets are ripping through them; at such times a hole in the ground is worth many tents. A reverie descends. Township tents form the base while bar boy's cocked beneath the stench of his canvas cover. His tent lies on the imaginary border of revolution and terror (rhetorical and real). Say it: the cusp of cold war's capital keeps the kettle hot. The focus shifts, the pedantic looms and, sure, white guilt's a bore, but look out, here she comes, a fantasy shanty-town some dreamt was more than just a symbol since divestment really happened. But what reality gets divested of meaning in this tiny victory, and again in juxtaposing these images? There's no place to dig a hole in Crossroads when the kaspirs come, so who can say to *faire une trou*[16] when we're so far apart. These tents are not commensurate.

In the mid-1970s, X million Black South Africans lived in shacks and tents.
In the mid 1980s, Y million Black South Africans lived in shacks and tents.
In the 2000s, Z million Black South Africans live in shacks and tents.

Athlone, 1982

Fighting on "the border," 1980s.

Crossroads, 1980s

Scenes from a Shantytown: Divestment movement encampment on the Arts Quad, 1986

"No one is suggesting that it is not the business of liberal whites to oppose what is wrong. However, it appears to us as too much of a coincidence that liberals—few as they are—should not only be determining the modus operandi of those blacks who oppose the system, but also leading it, in spite of their involvement in the system. To us it seems that their role spells out the totality of the white power structure—the fact that though whites are our problem, it is still other whites who want to tell us how to deal with that problem." Steve Biko, "Black Consciousness and the Quest for a True Humanity," in *I Write What I Like*.[17]

In *The Future of the Image,* Jacques Ranciere writes of what he terms dialectical montage and symbolic montage. "The dialectical way invests chaotic power in the creation of little machineries of the heterogeneous. By fragmenting continuums and distancing terms that call for each other, or conversely, by assimilating heterogeneous elements and combining incompatible things, it creates clashes... What is involved is revealing one world behind another: the far-off conflict behind home comforts."

"The symbolist way also relates heterogeneous elements and constructs little machines through a montage of unrelated elements. But it assembles them in accordance with the opposite logic. Between elements that are foreign to one another it works to establish a familiarity. [This machine] is a machine for making something common... To do two things at once: to organize a clash and construct a continuum. The space of these clashes and that of the continuum can even bear the same name: history."

Later, in the dance hall, the band takes a break. Intermission. The lights go down, then up again. It takes a minute to focus. White cardboard boater hats, sky blue satin jackets, bamboo canes, a troupe of dancers made up in whiteface with eyes and mouths ringed in maroon circles. I look at my cousin. She says, "Yeah. It's a coon show."

"South African public records show that white minstrel troupes were in Cape Town as early as the 1840s, and by the 1860s there were many troupes performing throughout the country."[18]

"While the creole culture [of the region] was developing through the interaction of people from varied origins, social conditions and beliefs, a new fad reached the Cape: American blackface minstrelsy. And with it the character of the Coon."[19]

"Members apply make-up to their face. Some stick to the old minstrel pattern: black with white circles around the eyes and mouth, or a variation on it."[20]

"Most members and captains of Cape Town's Coon troupes are not aware of the origin of the word; to them it means just what they are—people playing carnival in a costumed band. They ignore the American meaning of the word, and its racist connotations."[21]

A Cape Colored "Coon Carnival." A minstrel show. Jazz dance moves in rhythmic lines, hips synchronized to the electronic pulse. Mostly on the beat, but sometimes torn, a rag. A punch before you're ready, then the heart skips a beat. The optics are a blinder. Black skins, white masks may phantom a negative image, but what is really happening here? I can never read this. *I had not the great advantage of working over familiar ground.*

"When minstrel shows became commercialized at a later stage, they ossified racial stereotypes and became the vehicles of scorn, contempt, and derision against blacks. In order to understand why they became so popular among all groups of the South African population in the second half of the nineteenth century, it is nevertheless necessary to emphasize that their initial contents were mixed, anti-authoritarian, imbued with youth and working class rebellions; that the music, the dancing and even the acting they staged resulted from a complex cultural miscegenation."[22]

"Anticipated bass is a bass tone that comes syncopated shortly before the downbeat, which is used in Son montuno Cuban dance music... Another type of syncopation is the missed beat, in which a rest is substituted for an expected note's beginning. For example, if the musician suddenly does not play anything on beat 1, that would also be syncopation. Playing a note ever-so-slightly before or after a beat is another form of syncopation because this produces an unexpected accent."[23]

Reverse blackface transposes nothing to or from the dancers' smiles, their apparent joy in the synchronous motion. They're a regiment, a chorus line, a blast. Their fractal dance kaleidoscopes a pattern, an order and some chaos. A glance and a grimace from my cousin says don't misunderstand this infectious elation of dancers surging to the audience clapping and screaming for more. Hypnotic mayhem.

"'Tariek' perhaps explains more precisely what the [Coon] festivals are about.... In the language of Islam, more specifically of Sufi Islam, 't'ariqa' means 'the way', that is, the path leading to God, and the spiritual techniques which allow one to accomplish this journey.... 'Tariek', then, describes the trance-like state reached by participants... "According to Gerald Stone, who for many years studied the dialect of Afrikaans spoken by working-class coloured people living in the Cape Penninsula, 'tariek' means excitement, being carried away or being in a trance-like state. 'Tariek' is closely related to 'deurmekaar' [crazy, confused, silly] and consequently also connotes being mixed up and in a state of anomy."[24]

Anomy, anomie: a feeling of disorientation and alienation from society caused by the perceived absence of a supporting social or moral framework.

The dance and brandy dizzy, my eyes drift closed, but I should say I had a fantastic time. *The locality was totally new to me.* A memory jams the narrative. White light on the rug. My white-haired father holding my tiny baby in his big hands for the first time. The baby is fussy. My father rubs its bare pink belly. *This produces an unexpected accent.* He looks up, startled, and breaks into song in a thick Yorkshire accent:

> "My Egyptian mum-mum-mum-mum-mummy
> used to rub my tum-tum-tum-tum-tummy
> beneath the waving palm."

The baby stops crying. My father says, "I haven't thought of that since I was six years old and saw a group of men singing on the pier at Filey. In Pierrot hats. White with black pom-poms. In blackface."

"Whites get satisfaction in supposing the 'racial' Other enjoys in ways unavailable to them—through exotic food, strange and noisy music, outlandish bodily exhibitions, or unremitting sexual appetite. And yet at the same time, because the Other personifies their inner divisions, hatred of their own excess of enjoyment necessitates hatred of the Other." Eric Lott, *Love and Theft; Blackface Minstrelsy and the American Working Class.*[25]

"Which is to say that white subjectivity, founded on this splitting, was and is (in the words of Stallybrass and White) a 'mobile, conflictual fusion of power, fear and desire' (5) absolutely dependent on the Otherness it seeks to exclude and constantly open to transgression, although, in wonderfully adaptive fashion, even the transgression may be pleasurable."[26]

Timeline with gaps: In the 19th century, some whites, like the Christy Minstrels, put on blackface and imitated black songs and dances for paying audiences in the US and abroad. Then, some blacks in the U.S., like William Henry Lane (or Master Juba) or the Virginia Jubilee Singers, "black-up" to imitate themselves being imitated, After seeing them, mixed-race individuals in South Africa put on blackface in imitation. A little while later, white, Jewish, Lithuanian-American Al Jolson plays a white Jew in black face. Later still, my father watches white working-class Brits in blackface on the beach entertaining other working class whites. Today, the Colored South Africans in whiteface I am watching are in some way tied to all of them.

make the sequence of the whole intelligible. Trace it back. Start now. Colored [Africa]. Black over white over black over white over black, black over black over white over black, black over white over black, black over white, black [US], black [Africa]. So, these "coons" are mimicking whites mimicking blacks or blacks mimicking whites mimicking blacks or maybe even whites mimicking blacks mimicking whites mimicking blacks? Yes. Maybe. The mockery is multiple. Surely both master and slave take a beating. Or maybe neither.

"…minstrelsy as a safely imitative form: the notion of the black dancer 'imitating himself' indicates minstrelsy's fundamental consequence for black culture, the dispossession and control by whites of black forms that would not for a long time be recovered…. [In] this simulacral dilemma… It was hard to see the real thing without being reminded, even unfavorably, of the copy, the 'cover version' that effectively did its work of cultural coverage. Nor, just as surely, could the copy be seen without reminding one of the real thing."[27]

Maybe the question is when does any of this, as Ellison famously asked, change the joke and slip the yoke? Or where? Or for whom? It is important to remember that in South Africa, these shows were traditionally performed primarily by and for the colored community. But here, in the town hall, performing for whites, the relation's oddly altered. What was happening back when Colored South Africans first mimicked the American "coon"? Were they longing for a different kind of blackness? An American blackness that was, post-Civil War, freer? Was there the appeal of yet another Other, the American black as exotically familiar—at once recognizable and different? And how does the twist of whiteface signify? Is it the white of whiteness or a clownface whiteness? Historians note that whites have traditionally been mocked in these shows. What does it mean to see this show here in post-apartheid's supposed "rainbow nation," here in this enclave of white power where the performers are paid to amuse, where even if the enjoyment of both audience and performers is real, the performers are still so easily mocked by the watchers, so thoroughly consumed by the economic hierarchies still in place? And how does it connect to the days when these same white people, and their parents before them, might only have seen "coons" dance while visiting colored neighborhoods with their nannies. Those moments when the nannies took their charges home with them. My mother talks of the pleasure of going to the colored beach with her nanny, to the colored movie theatre, to eat special food in Nanny's neighborhood at Ramadan. An early childhood pleasure of otherness tied up with the maternal safety of the nanny? So now, who, if anyone, is degraded by this spectacle? Maybe only the ones who read it as complicit with racial oppression. Maybe only those apart from this society.

Later, on a "township tour," I see black women in chalky, watery white-face. "Our" "guide" tells me it is it is to keep off the sun; someone else tells me it is tribal. *Make the sequence of the whole intelligible.* How to look backward and forward through backsight forethought. O Janus-faced angel blowing through the fucked-up satire of a military text still used as a straight guide. A coon show is both exploitative and subversive. Or neither. This is some duffer's drift.

"Thought of the Other is sterile without the other of Thought.

Thought of the Other is the moral generosity disposing me to accept the principle of alterity, to conceive of the world as not simple and straightforward, with only one truth—mine. But thought of the Other can dwell within me without making me alter course, without 'prizing me open,' without changing me within myself. An ethical principle, it is enough that I not violate it.

The other of Thought is precisely this altering. Then I have to act. That is the moment I change my thought, without renouncing its contribution. I change, and I exchange. This is the aesthetics of turbulence whose corresponding ethics is not provided in advance.

If, thus, we allow that an aesthetics is an art of conceiving, imagining and acting, the other of Thought is the aesthetics implemented by me and by you to join the dynamics to which we are to contribute." Edouard Glissant, *Poetics of Relation.*

Loaded. Tanked. Pissed. Dead drunk return from the dance to my aunt's house. In bed in the pink room, lips buzz. Taste blood in the corner. Morning. Slatted shuttered windows. Beyond, blood red poinsettias from ground to sky. Irrational roots, pinwheels, hats, and flames choked by indigo morning glories, white centers sharp stars. Soon, the gardener comes in royal blue overalls, bends to cut the lawn with clippers no bigger than scissors. For breakfast: pawpaw. To get to the cool salmon-colored flesh, cut the wrinkled hide of skin, then scoop out wads of slimy seeds smelling vaguely of vomit.

Minstrelsy. "Selves into others, and back again"[28]

A Different Smell

> To articulate the past historically does not mean to recognize it 'the way it really was'. It means to seize hold of a memory as it flashes up in a moment of danger.
>
> —Walter Benjamin, *Illuminations*

We are back in the U.S., driving in a metallic blue mini-van. A rental. My small, dark-haired mother; my muscular, triathlete sister-in-law, Heather; my two toddler nephews; my two children and I are packed in among the granola bars, the coffee cups, the plastic containers of matchbox cars and broken crayons. Trip trash.

The soundtrack for *Oklahoma* is playing and my mother and sister-in-law are singing along.

When we hit that road, hell-for-leather. Cats and dogs will dance in the heather. Don't you wish you'd go on forever? Don't you wish you'd go on forever? Don't you wish you'd go on forever? And you'd never stop?

I am in the passenger seat, looking out at miles of sagebrush and trying to go unconscious. I have a brief, happy dream of a deep orange prescription pill bottle. I think of the word *amber*, then *ambergris*. Resin and intestines. People will make jewels filled with ancient junk, bugs. People will make perfume from a stinking, gray, waxy mass expelled from whale guts.

I am making you this story.

I am brought back by the sound of my mother and Heather singing along melodramatically to "Poor Jud is Dead." My mother stops suddenly and says,

"Oh."

She has just remembered something from her childhood in South Africa. Each year, she and her best friend, Wendy, would get to go to a musical in Cape Town. There, they'd see the show, buy the record, take it home and play it all summer long, learning the lyrics.

One year, *Annie Get Your Gun*. And they spent their days by the ocean at Hermanus, clambering over the rocks, like the baboons above them, down to the beaches. One beach thick with the crunch of navy-blue mussel shells where they'd search for the few buried pink ones, pink like the inside of their mouths, smooth glimpses of pale flesh hidden in the blue black. One beach littered with brown kelp tubes. Long, rubbery intestines of seaweed to be put to use as sand castle drainage pipes. One beach an infinite avenue of wide white and wind, cutting a swath through blue blue. Sky, mountains, pounding sea. And everywhere they sang,

Oh you can't get a man with a gun. Oh my mother was frightened by a shotgun they say. That's why I'm such a wonderful shot. I'd be out in the cactus and I'd practice all day. And now tell me what have I got. Oh a man may be hot, but he's not when he's shot. Oh you can't get a man with a gun with a gun with a gun.

No. You can't get a man with a gun.

"I was about nine or ten," my mother says, "maybe 1946." The year Steve Biko was born.

Two years later, it was *Oklahoma*.

Oh, what a beautiful mornin'. Oh, what a beautiful day. I've got a beautiful feelin'. Everything's goin' my way.

1948. The word apartheid is coined. The National Party's election-year promise to institutionalize racism. The year my mother and Wendy were singing,

We know we belong to the land. And the land we belong to is grand!

One night, at dusk, they went to bed in their cots on the sleeping porch, under the thatched roof that smelled like a damp barn, wet sand, a rotting marsh. There was the usual sound of waves, the enormity of the sea hidden beyond a grove of scrubby milkwood bushes. But they couldn't sleep, so they walked, in their pajamas, to the point above Langbai. On the way, they passed a man, a black man. They said hello. He said he was waiting for Wendy's maid.

At this point in the story, I get nervous. I know this is the point to start worrying. Not about the little girls, but about that man.

The next morning, a neighbor came up on the porch and said, "There's a dead man in the bushes."

Of course. Of course there was.

"We ran to see, even though the grownups were saying, 'No. No,'" my mother says. "We were excited."

And, of course, it was the same man. Dead. Later, the girls heard that the maid said she was with this man when her husband showed up and grew angry and stabbed him.

My mother and Wendy were punished for looking by being made to stay indoors all day. Where they sang, "Poor Jud is Dead" over and over and over. For which they were punished again.

He's lookin' oh so purty and so nice. He looks like he's asleep, It's a shame that he won't keep. But it's summer and we're running out of ice.

In the van, it is quiet now. The littlest children are sleeping. I am driving. Lulled. Just staying in my lane. The sky is dark and there is rain as we cross the continental divide and pass the turnoff for the Apache reservation. I turn away. We are almost home.

I ask my mother if she saw other bodies, later, or if she knew of other killings, political killings. She says, no. "No, we were so sheltered. But, we heard of them." I ask, "Not even when you worked in the townships, later?" She shakes her head.

I think of my mother as a child in Africa. Sheltered. Not sheltered. I wonder when the innocence of those white childhoods ended and when denial or complicity or escape or resistance became choices. I think of how the question of choice is always so buried by privilege. How the smooth road we're on pulls us so relentlessly. How my mother's life looks one way when I think of her as the girl in our family photo albums. And another in the light of history. And how I always see that history in the light of my mother.

Later I'll look up the lyrics to "Poor Jud is Dead" and find the original ones paired with a common mishearing.

The original lyrics read: *The daisies in the dell. Will give out a different smell.*

The misunderstood ones say: *The days he's in the dell. We'll give out a different smell.*

approaching eyes will see only what I'm supposed to write, my dar —
keywords South Africa's legacy a narcotizing mix of electoral democracy, multi-culturalism, despair, inequity and material conditions unchanged, crimes unpunished, all the things to write,
but not coming to the conclusion that reconciliations hegemony
must be interrogated, so that the sjambok of the past can still
sting. No heliotrope here.

"Twenty Questions"

> The fact of the matter is that nationalism thinks in terms of historical destinies, while racism dreams of eternal contaminations, transmitted from the origins of time through an endless sequence of loathsome copulations: outside history.
>
> —Benedict Anderson, *Imagined Communities*

We are in the mini-van again. We are playing a version of "Twenty Questions" called "Who Am I?" We are guessing identities. It is my nephew's turn. He's in first grade. He's a tow-headed blond with bright blue eyes like his mother. The game has been going on too long and we are impatient. "We give up. Who are you?" He refuses; makes us keep guessing.

Here's what we know: he's a man, he's not a character in a book, he's not a movie star, he's not dead, he's black, and yes, we all know his name. We call out everyone we can think of. We've been driving a long time. Finally, he says, "Okay, okay I'll tell you." And then, with a big grin of victory, "I'm my dad!"

There is a long silence in the car. Someone says, "Your dad's black?" and Quinn says "Yeah!" Two syllables, like "duh-uh." His mother says, "Oh, hun, your dad's not black, he's just really tan." Another pause.

His dad says, "Well, it's more complicated than that." Another silence. His grandfather says, "Ah, the question of Chuck's negritude." Somebody changes the topic.

I look at Quinn who, up until now, in the spring of first grade, thought his father was black. But just this minute learned that it was not so simple. Will he remember this day? Will he remember that he had a black father? Or will he forget and assimilate? I want to know the nuances of his racial identity or identities, but I know my family is tired of my obsession and I don't want to interfere with their own family dynamic. Still, I desperately want to grill him and his brother. The two of them are mirrors for my brother and me as children—me as white as can be and Chuck so dark my mother used to say, "There must be some black blood in there somewhere."

My mother grew up dark-skinned enough in South Africa that she was often warned not to spend too much time in the sun because otherwise she'd have to go to the colored beach. A nice catch: stay out of the sun so you can keep your access to the white beach, to which you can't go because the sun there will turn you black.

For a while I would tell Quinn's identity story any chance I got, insinuating, and enjoying, the possibilities of my own blackness. But then I read Nadine Gordimer's story "Beethoven Was One-Sixteenth Black" in which she takes white South Africans to task for finding their one drop of black blood as yet another way to lay claim to power.

———————

Race, power, class. In South Africa, apartheid was always about power and race, but also always about class oppression, an oppression that was primarily economic, about property and poverty, and in some ways, race was the ruse. Race was the way of enforcing power relations and at the same time a way of disguising it. As Benedict Anderson writes, "The dreams of racism actually have their origin in ideologies of class, rather than in those of nation: above all in claims to divinity among rulers and to 'blue' or 'white' blood and 'breeding' among aristocracies." Not that the racism and race hatred wasn't real. It was. Only that discussions that focus solely on racial difference rather than economic exploitation miss a central aspect of apartheid's program and that precisely this "mistake" was made at the time apartheid was dismantled, so that its end may have meant the end of the ruse of racism—the end of race as the legal category of exploitation—but the abysmal material conditions of the majority of people living in South Africa were left untouched.

Yes, positions of political power are no longer held solely by whites. Yes, there is an emerging black middle class and a black upper class. Yes, people of all colors now have access to the top end of inequality, but inequality and poverty persist. Yes, people are no longer forcibly made to live in distant "homelands," but how many thousands are still forced into labor-based dislocations and migrations? If racial egalitarianism doesn't result in economic egalitarianism, the end of apartheid might be both "good" (or "just") and ineffectual. The struggle merely shifts.

Mandela and the ANC knew this, but they came to power at a particular historical moment that radically shaped and weakened their victory—a moment at the end of communism, at the triumph of neo-liberal capitalism when the ANC's economic program did not seem tenable. Some argue that when the ANC achieved racial equality, they dropped the true, economic, struggle, because they could suddenly profit. But this doesn't mean that their victory was a hollow one. That would be a cynicism we can't afford.

I don't want to be a cynic. I want the utopian moment of South Africa's transition to persist. I want the fantasy of the rainbow nation. I want the multi-racial debates in the Cape Town flower market to continue. I want the will to struggle. I want the struggle for economic justice to prevail. And I want my nephew to be neither black nor white. Or both.

at night, there is a continent below me. The light is different. Yellow and watery like children's urine. Tire fires still smolder. Mountains hang upside down, pendulous blue lobes. The sea splashes down on my face when I look north. The Southern Cross is nothing etched in air, but once, by accident, a lunar eclipse like a slow amber bruise. Too slow. The world really was ending and no one was there to explain it. Some were dancing at a wedding behind me. Late night white men with burnished faces drunkenly incanting, *How can we dance when the world is turning?* The throb and their chorus. I close my eyes behind the security system.

V. Cape Town Journals II

Graffiti

"Freedom Day" was cancelled. My cousin said, "Ach, shame man." They say that a lot here. All the time. *Ach, shame.* It means something like, "what a pity," but here, shame resonates.

My cousin said, "Come on, we'll drive out to Christmas Camp," a campsite in the mountains where generations of our family's names are painted on an enormous boulder. A place for filiation and belonging. Home. Family. Nation. Longing for belonging. Longing to leave it behind. Is belonging to a family like belonging to a nation? Maybe only if one adheres to a worldview wherein families are made by blood and being a citizen is simply what you are by birth, rather than a status symbolic of certain rights and values.

My cousin said, "We can drive past Victor Verster and Pollsmor—the prisons where your Uncle John was. And Mandela too." As if they were linked. Or maybe as if one will cancel out the other.

All of my cousins say, "You should come back. You're really African. Your children should be in Africa." Note, not, "South Africa," but "Africa"—that utopian consolidation of the continent. While I think, post-apartheid, they might finally be able to begin to share Robert Sobukwe's Pan Africanist dream, I suspect that for them this imagined unity outside national boundaries is, unlike his, depoliticized and ahistorical. And I suspect my family's vision retains more than whiff of white colonial domination. My family wants me to correct course, put our lineage back on the map where it has been since the 1600s. This seems both absurd and powerful. To be African seems exotic and liberating. It would free me from being American without having to become "South" African. I imagine "returning" to one past and leaving another behind; to belong and to be free of belonging. Intoxicating. The fact that all around me a *National Geographic* special is being projected—the grass waving golden green, the blue gum tress swishing in slo-mo, the sky blue and yellow, the fields full of ibis, even the glamour of the recent struggle still shining just out of the frame—makes me dizzy.

————

George Oppen: "We are not coeval / with a locality / But we imagine others are."

————

"Are there modes of belonging that can be rigorously non-nationalistic?" This is the one question Judith Butler says Hannah Arendt poses in her 1951 book, *The Origins of Totalitarianism.* Butler responds:

> I think it has to be the case, because the critique of nationalism is so profound, and yet she wants to maintain this right of belonging, at least at this stage in her thinking. What can this right of belonging be?....one thing we seem to know is that she does not want that rule of law to be bound by a nation, a national group, a national majority, even a national minority. If the state she wants is a nation-state at all it would be a nation-state that would be rigorously opposed to a nationalism and, hence, a nation-state that would have to nullify itself as such. If the community she wants and the modes of belonging she is in favor of are to have any meaning for her in this framework, they would be rigorously non-nationalist. She does not tell us what they might be, but I think she poses that question: what would non-nationalist modes of belonging be? I'm not sure she is describing reality as it is, but making use of language to invoke, incite, and solicit a different future.

Slipping from possible futures, to the present, to the past, we drive out of Cape Town as the radio plays "Freedom Day" special reports and the national anthem drifts in and out.

Gayatri Chakravorti Spivak in conversation with Judith Butler in *Who Sings the Nation State? Language, Politics, Belonging* says that the national anthem must be sung in the national language. She writes, "The nation-state requires the national language....the language of the anthem cannot be negotiated."

And yet, South Africa has seventeen official national languages, five of which are in the national anthem. Still, perhaps this is just one particularly vivid example of how the "new" South Africa is both utopia and dystopia. A new, multi-cultural nation with a famously progressive constitution where millions live in shanty-towns that run along the shamefully beautiful perimeters of the gated garden estates. The anthem includes so many more than before, but cannot extend to everyone.

Official Lyrics of the South African National Anthem

Nkosi sikelel' iAfrika   [Xhosa and Zulu]
Maluphakanyisw' uphondo lwayo,
Yizwa imithandazo yethu,
Nkosi sikelela, thina lusapho lwayo.

Morena boloka setjhaba sa heso,   [Sesotho]
O fedise dintwa le matshwenyeho,
O se boloke, O se boloke setjhaba sa heso,
Setjhaba sa South Afrika - South Afrika.

Uit die blou van onse hemel,   [Afrikaans]
Uit die diepte van ons see,
Oor ons ewige gebergtes,
Waar die kranse antwoord gee,

Sounds the call to come together,   [English]
And united we shall stand,
Let us live and strive for freedom,
In South Africa our land.[29]

———————

We drive. My cousin tells me family stories.

"Your Uncle John, he was this gangster, glamorous and illicit. We called him 'double oh seven' or 'Goldfinger.' He had two Mercedes. He'd breeze in, larger than life, laughing, magnanimous. You never knew what to believe. You'd hear things. He's trading for the government. He's dealing diamonds. He carried a suitcase with twenty or so tags. He was so proud of his travels in Africa. Once I saw a cover article on him. The picture showed him with one foot on the step of a private jet. They painted him as a legitimate businessman. But you know, there were scams.

I remember once being at the sea with the family and two guys in suits coming onto the beach and talking to John and asking for the keys to his car. There were scams. I don't know the details. I think he got pension fund money and lost it. Maybe he bribed them. I think he got two years that time. I remember the first time he came out of jail. This would have been the late '70s or early '80s. At a friend's wedding the band played "Jail House Rock" and people were saying "Check out John," looking for a reaction. I doubt they got one. Once, later on, I saw him being chauffeured in a tiny Toyota. He was in the back with a chauffer up front."

"Look," my cousin says as we get out beyond the suburbs, past vineyards and farmland, "this is the point where the new road ended and you had to swerve off to get on the old road. John was fiddling with the radio and he went through the barrier with his big Merc and your aunt went through the window. The legend is that she was saved by her fur coat. This would have been 1970, '71, '72."

———

This would have been 1970, '71, '72.

In 1970, The Bantu Homelands Citizenship Act stripped blacks of their South African citizenship. It required all black individuals to become citizens of a self-governing territorial authority. As Minister Connie Mulder stated: "No black person will eventually qualify in terms of section 10 because they will all be aliens, and as such, will only be able to occupy the houses bequeathed to them by their fathers, in the urban areas, by special permission of the Minister," i.e., black people are forced to reside in designated "homeland" areas, made citizens of that homeland, and denied South African nationality and the right to work in South Africa. Every "African" is issued with a certificate of citizenship of his respective "homeland."

As one report stated, "A man cannot become the occupier of a township house, nor even arrange for his wife to be transferred from another prescribed area, in which she qualifies, to suitable accommodation which he can offer her in the Peninsula, until he can show that he is the registered citizen of a Homeland. 'I have become a foreigner in my own country' was said by one, and many have commented no less poignantly, so much for 'separate freedoms.'"[30]

In 1970, the term "black consciousness" enters the discourse of the South African Students' Organization. In August, in an article published in SASO's newsletter, Steve Biko writes: "The integration they (white liberals) talk about is… a one-way of course, with the Whites doing all the talking and the Blacks the listening…. The myth of integration as propounded under the banner of liberal ideology must be cracked and killed because it makes people believe that something is being done when in actual fact the artificial integrated circles are a soporific on the blacks and provide a vague satisfaction for the guilty-stricken whites." Biko says that Sekou Toure was right when he wrote, "To take part in the African revolution, it is not enough to write a revolutionary song; you must fashion the revolution with the people. And if you fashion it with the people, the songs will come of themselves."

In the 1970's Walter Sisulu's informal lectures on the ANC, held while he and other prisoners worked in the lime quarry on Robben Island, formed the major component of a fully-fledged course of study known as "Syllabus A" that included two years of lectures about the ANC and the liberation struggle, a course on the Indian struggle, a history of the coloured people, and a course on Marxism.

In 1970, in a Declaration on the 25th anniversary of the United Nations, the General Assembly described apartheid as "a crime against the conscience and dignity of mankind."

———

In 1971, The United Nations General Assembly asked all world govern-
ments to apply a full-scale embargo on arms supplies to South Africa
and condemned the establishment of Bantustans or 'homelands.'

In 1971, The International Court of Justice at The Hague declared that
South Africa was under obligation to withdraw its administration from
Namibia immediately and thus put an end to its occupation of the territory. John Vorster reacted by indicating that as the judgment was only
advisory, it could not be considered binding, and South Africa would
act as it saw fit.

———

In 1972, the South African Police (SAP) deploy to Namibia.

In 1972, Ahmed Timol, a political detainee, was killed in jail five days
after his arrest. A sixteen-day inquest at the Regional Court in Johannesburg concludes that he "fell" to his death from the tenth floor of a
building while in police custody. They say he committed suicide and
nobody is held accountable.[31]

———

In *The Memory of Birds in Times of Revolution*, Breyten Breytenbach
writes:

I have come to the stage where I don't want you to talk about Apartheid unless you also recognize how it flows from our shared history, how it dovetails with elements of your ideologies and sentiments, and how talking about it can morally neutralize the unimaginable horror of it. I refuse to continue being a party to the condemnation of Apartheid, which leads only to moral posturing. We are fattening the monster on our outcries of shame.

———

My cousin drives us up into the mountains on a long ochre road. To our left is a big black rock—a rock the size of a small town, hundreds of feet high. The stone bulges like brains. Its three main lobes each have different names and are scarred by huge grooves left by dripping water. When dry, it is a pale, elephant gray with the greenish tinge of lichen; when wet, it glistens blackly.

We find the camp. The official "Christmas Camp / Krismaskamp" park sign reads:

"During the first decade of this century, Paarl Mt. was the holiday resort of various groups of Paarlites.... Their necessities were transported by horse-drawn wagon. Horses, milk cows, suckling pigs, chickens for slaughter and a keg of beer were all part of the trek. Each family's tent had a site under the large wild olive trees. Many nails in the trunks of the trees still indicate where the kitchen tent was located. Horse riding, jukskei, and a large fire at night, were among the most important pastimes.

In 1908 the beautiful campsite was christened Christmas Camp and the large bell and the date were printed on the rock. The names of the children who were born were added to the list on the rock every year. This 'family register' which could initially have been considered graffiti, has over the years become part of the 'cultural history' of Paarl Mountain and as such is protected.

VISITORS ARE REQUESTED TO KINDLY REFRAIN FROM PAINTING OR WRITING ON THE ROCKS. SUCH ACTIONS WILL BE CONSIDERED A SERIOUS TRANSGRESSION.

———

There are two families picnicking under the trees. One speaks Afrikaans, the other English, both are white. A guy comes up and asks what we're doing. He tells us about some graffiti in a cave made by former Prime Minister D.F. Malan. He says, "I'm ashamed he was a graffitist. I'm a Malan too, distantly related." I ask him if he's more ashamed that Malan was a graffitist or the "father of apartheid"? "Acch," he says, "We would all like to claim now that it wasn't us. We didn't do it. Anyway, I'm not a *close* relative."

On an exposed patch of rock in the center of the site, "XMAS CAMP" is painted in big white letters. A giant white bell separates the words. One family's names form a column on one side; the other list flanks it. I see the names of my great grandparents, my grandparents, great uncles and aunts, some cousins. And there, to the side, near a part that has been painted over, in small capital letters, someone has painted the word "shame."

bad family's a cancer or a cause, celebration's inevitable denial flaunts misdeed and even evil cleans its teeth in the mirror of not me, not my people. Claims can't corroborate or be made for maids and nanny's not talking now except to say, *those were happy, happy days, so long ago* and *I can't understand any of you*. Language haunted by history. Languages haunted by histories. Up the ante on your etymologies. Grammar may be a structure of domination's nation, but just because it sutures subject to object or predicate or property doesn't mean disruptions jump the fence with any consequence. Maybe vernacular's an agent of unruliness, or maybe its in the swing between verse and chorus of writing as praxis. Adorno's Deutsch cracks the code and Esperanto's whacked dream to make a necessary mash-up of internationalisms that cleaves language between itselves. That's the polyphonic shit you crave. *Language as both bond and division.* Wracked syntax a revolution won't engender, but at least, Ariadne, there's a thread from boredom's doom. Patience. *All this hearing and being heard takes time.* From chaos to story and back is meaning's green oscillation.

Shame

Shame and guilt twist around each other. They writhe. At times in their spiral, they distinguish themselves, at times they blur.

In post-apartheid South Africa, especially following the work of the Truth and Reconciliation Commission, questions of guilt and shame arise repeatedly—not just questions of juridical guilt, but of guilty feelings. Sometimes, these are quickly, and perhaps rightly, dismissed. "Who cares about white guilt?" But they are also a locus of inquiry.

"Guilt is such a useless thing… guilt immobilizes you. 'I am guilty—so what can I do?'" says Nomfundo Walaza, who was the Executive Director of the Trauma Centre for Survivors of Violence and Torture in South Africa. Walaza is quoted in Antjie Krog's examination of the Truth and Reconciliation Commission, *Country of My Skull*, saying, "Feelings of guilt are also open to abuse by those who suffered: 'You are guilty—so give me a thousand rand.' I prefer shame. Because when you feel shame about something you really want to change it, because it is not comfortable to sit with shame." Several years after this, Walaza tells me, "The more we talk about shame, the more we'll understand forgiveness. It is easier to forgive someone expressing shame. You can see shame."

People in South Africa often seem to use the words guilt and shame interchangeably, as synonyms, or, just as often, as radically different from one another. Walaza's approach is fairly common among academics. We can hear a similar take in Jacqueline Rose's essay "Apathy and Accountability: The Challenge of South Africa's Truth and Reconciliation Commission to the Intellectual in the Modern World" in *On Not Being Able to Sleep*, where she writes, "Unlike guilt, which can fester quietly inside you, shame only arises when someone knows, or fears, they have been seen." Sometimes people I spoke with would associate guilt with religious discourse and shame with ethics, sometimes not. Sometimes guilt was bad (i.e. unproductive) and shame was not. Sometimes they were both dismissed as irrelevant. Usage often seemed muddled.

This is not all that surprising given the history of the terms. According to Ruth Leys in her book *From Guilt to Shame; Auschwitz and After*, "From the start of the twentieth century until the early 1960s, shame was rarely differentiated from guilt, appearing instead as a minor variant of the latter." Leys describes a "general shift that has taken place in the course of the last forty years from a discourse of guilt to a discourse of shame." Today, says Leys, "shame (and shamelessness) has displaced guilt as a dominant emotional reference in the West." Leys details the transformation of shame from a negative to a "potentially positive" position, explaining that,

> Writers now make guilt shame's 'other,' the carrier of bad, negative, and destructive implications, while identifying shame as more productive, even possibly healing, in its very nature. More precisely, although shame is often characterized in terms of inadequacy, lack, or failure in relation to some personal ideal or standard, it is also widely perceived to contain a positive component.

Crucial in the shift Leys makes from historiography to critique is her observation that most recent shame theorists share a commitment to "anti-intentionalism, materialism, and the primacy of personal identity or difference." Leys says that this shifts our focus from shame as a response to 'what you have done' to a focus on shame as an expression of 'who you are.' She finds this shift "unsound," and she's quite convincing if we are seeking routes for change. We can change what we do more easily than we can change who we are.

And yet, Leys' formulation doesn't quite translate when we consider the context of the oppressor's shame, rather than the victim's. For instance, when Leys writes, "What is crucially at stake in the current tendency to replace guilt with shame is an impulse to displace questions about our moral responsibility for what we do in favor of more ethically neutral or different questions about our personal attributes." This seems to be the reverse of the post-apartheid scene in South Africa where the focus on shame is a call for ethical responsibility, for retributive action. In South Africa, what is wanted from the oppressors is an expression of shame as a personal emotion stemming from the guilt of having committed misdeeds. In other words, one's *juridical* guilt should be made manifest in a bodily shame that reveals itself through a particular affect or public expression.

This linking of the juridical and the emotional was central to the discourse surrounding the Truth and Reconciliation Commission. For an interesting take on the function of such national projects, Leys turns to the work of Sara Ahmed, who according to Leys explores "how national declarations of shame for past wrongs not only play a role in the process of reconciliation, but can bring national identity into existence by subordinating notions of individual guilt and responsibility to the collective." As an exercise in nation building, or in the reinvention of nations that is possible during a radical transitional, this seems productive, but the turn to the collective can both a) leave unresolved the question of how nations might productively "use" shame for change in order to accomplish something material such as land or wealth distribution, and b) let individual responsibility off the hook. Leys notes that Ahmed addresses the latter when she suggests that

> The desire to feel better through the public discourse of shame displaces the recognition of injustice. In other words, the apology functions as a technique for producing national identity for

its members as individuals who feel shame yet also 'feel better,' and it does so by forestalling debate over what harms have been done, who or what has been responsible, and the nature of the injustice.

When I spoke with Nomfundo Walaza, she addressed both issues, saying,

> I worry often about the fact that there hasn't been justice for many individuals. Even without the justice, there's the fact that reparations and rehabilitation could have been done. And this would have compensated people in some way. There were some individuals who felt 'Okay fine, you know these guys have to be pardoned by the state because of politics. I've got to forgive and whatever, but at least, you know, make sure that my life is better. Acknowledge it by actually giving me something. Give me something to educate the children that I'm now left with. Give me something to educate myself. Give me something to change my life. Do something so that I can also be counted among the human beings of this country.' I think the fact that reparations and rehabilitation has been dragged on, have never really been paid, has complicated the whole notion of justice. For me justice is not only the court part of justice, it is also the justice that would have come as a result of reparations and rehabilitation being given in time, so that people felt that the acknowledgement was genuine, it wasn't just "Oh we've heard you, but you know what, we don't think you deserve to be taken away from your misery."

The shift from the individual to the collective, or the nation, means that we have to reconsider the meaning and possibilities of shame. Individuals can feel shame (or not) for acts they have committed and individuals can feel shame (or not) at acts committed by their collective, and each trajectory will shape their possible responses, but they will, necessarily, be individual responses. But can the collective, the nation, feel shame? Is the polis truly like a public body? Collectives exist and certainly condition individual responses, but at what point to we choose to name something a "collective action"? And does this bring us dangerously close to notions of a kind of "collective unconscious" about which, de Certeau reminds us that

> The ambiguities of these modes of interpretation have been vigor-
> ously criticized, most vehemently in the work of Michel Foucault.
> They essentially depend upon the uncertain status, neither fish nor
> fowl, of 'totalities' which are not legible on the surfaces of texts, but
> which lurk just beneath them, in the fashion of invisible realities
> that would uphold phenomena. How can we simply assume these
> unities, and how can they be spotted in the middle depths between
> consciousness and the economic realm? They assume the place of a
> 'collective spirit' and, as such, retain the trace of ontologism.

If we agree that collectives structure our experiences as individuals, but
also that they are not strictly analogous; in this instance, they cannot experience shame as individuals do, nor can they assume responsibility as
individuals do (South Africa cannot be ashamed, but South Africans can
engage in public discourses of apology, forgiveness, and reconciliation
without most of its individual citizens actually apologizing, forgiving,
or reconciling), then we are left with the question of if and how shame
might motivate the actions of individuals, whether shame can serve as a
lash or is merely a palliative.

One issue in addressing this question is the way the realms of the emotional, the ethical, and the juridical abut one another here and can con-
fuse the terms of the response. Leys unpacks this in her discussion of
Georgio Agamben's *Remnants of Auschwitz: The Witness and the Archive*,
particularly around his discussion of Primo Levi. Leys notes that Agamben "inisists on the need to distinguish between ethical and juridical
categories," on a "non-juridical element to truth," and on the position
that "notions of responsibility and guilt are irremediably contaminated
by law." What this means, Leys explains, is that for Agamben,

> The gesture of assuming responsibility is genuinely juridical and
> not ethical: it expresses 'nothing noble or luminous' (RA, 22) but

simply legal obligation. Responsibility and guilt thus express simply 'two aspects of legal imputability; it was only later that they were interiorized and moved outside the law. Hence the insufficiency and opacity of every ethical doctrine that claims to be founded on these two concepts.' (RA, 22). '.... he asserts that 'ethics is the sphere that recognizes neither guilt nor responsibility; it is, as Spinoza knew, the doctrine of the happy life. To assume guilt and responsibility—which can at times be necessary—is to leave the territory of ethics and enter that of law' (RA, 24).

Leys objects to this as a "an extremely—if not perversely—restrictive concept of guilt." While this may be true, for this vision makes the realm of ethics ethereally disconnected from the material, I was struck by the relevance, for South Africa, of Agamben's example of Eichmann pleading guilty "before God, not the law" and Agamben's claim that moral responsibility is valuable only when one also assumes legal responsibility.

Perhaps I should have begun this essay with the following image. This is a picture of a group of women who felt shame for the actions of their nation and acted on that shame. A group of women who felt their nation should change its laws to reflect a moral position, should align the juridical with the ethical. A group of women that briefly included my mother.

When I look at this photograph I feel both shame and pride.

nobody, who are you? A fucking nation? Walcott I'm not. A roseate universe, subcutaneous nipple, prismatic cd playing cum and dust and Oum Kalsoum. You are your nation, like it or not, a pacifier popped in your mouth at birth. National identity's inevitable as sand, as inescapable as blood, a dark juggernaut. MLK refused to accept despair as the only response to the ambiguities of history, but I can't, today, so far from you, O Canada, who is asked to represent it? Which I's slip the noose? Salim Halali's heart may have been a foreign country, mine's a minefield for you, *h'bibi*, skip the stones, centrifugal archipelago, ruin[32]

The Black Sash

The Black Sash (named for the sashes they wore to mourn the death of the constitution following the removal of Colored voting rights in 1955) was an organization begun by bourgeois white women who protested (in white gloves with placards and posters), organized boycotts and rallies, and saw little change. After a few years, they opened "Advice Offices" in the townships to try to help victims of apartheid resolve problems with their passes, obtain access to legal assistance, locate their dead.

The Black Sash says that they have "always kept these two perspectives in sight – the implications of laws and policies and the practical effects that these have on the lives of the poor." They spent their first forty years opposing apartheid and its unjust laws. Forty years of what they characterize as "persistent, apparently fruitless campaigning against the pass laws, forced removals, detention without trial, inequality and repression." On his release from prison, Nelson Mandela called them the "the conscience of white South Africa." The Black Sash focused on fixing the everyday problems of the system since they couldn't fix the system. Their archives reveal their own awareness of the ways in which they were at once ineffectual and humane, complicit and resistant, irrelevant and necessary.

Why listen to their stories? To learn from their successes and their failures? To use that knowledge now? To acknowledge their efforts? What was the value of those efforts? What else should they have done? What else could they have done? What should we do? What can we do? What will I do? Will it be enough?

Maybe I'm just looking for my mother. In this next picture, taken on Adderley Street, in Cape Town, I think I see her, a college student, in a little white hat.

Zooming in, I find myself looking for evidence that she did something in the face of state-based terror, looking to pull her out from the crowd, looking to excuse her from her history, and maybe me from mine. But no one is excused. And I know my mother's story. She was, and is, a good person. She attended rallies. But she was not a radical. She was a social worker and then an emigrant. A woman in a position to leave. Still, these are documents of dissent.

I find myself wondering if looking at all this is a distraction from looking at the real suffering of the majority? But the next box of photos includes this one:

Who is on the outside and who is on the inside at once clear and troubled.

The archives are layered with evidence of many lives—the documented and the documenters. Sometimes, the documents are covered with disturbing personal eruptions in the margins—exclamation marks, expressions of dismay, decorative doodles—written by those trying, and failing, to stop oppression from within the system. Throughout, there are signs of struggle, boredom, hope, effort, fatigue, tedium, privilege, its lack, brutality, tyranny, complicity, despair, and resistance.

BOX A3
ADVICE OFFICE REPORT
May 1972

"The whole structure of pass laws and influx control makes it impossible for normal economic factors to regulate employer-worker relationships. The law deprives African employees of their human rights and demands much of them. Justice demands much of employers who have to operate in such a system."

BOX A3
ADVICE OFFICE REPORT
June 1972

"It seems that the Black Sash was rather naïve in February when it welcomed Dr. Koornhof's announcement that a man qualifying to live permanently in an urban area might bring his wife to live with him in terms of Section 10(1)(c) of the Urban Areas Act."

This passage from an internal report by the Black Sash is followed by pages and pages of explanation about how Koornhof's promise was thwarted by the bureaucracy. The document concludes,

"No, it seems, there is no hope."

BOX A3
April and May 1974

"Mr. Punt Janson, the Deputy Minister of Bantu Administration, was quoted in the press last week as saying
'To talk about family housing for these people would
be to merely profess one's own ignorance as to what
family life is to the Bantu." In the experience of all
the workers in the Black Sash offices, family life to
African people means just the same as it does to everyone else - security, love, companionship, warmth and
stability in which to raise one's children and, if this
is to profess our ignorance, then we suggest that the
Deputy Minister asks a few of the husbands and wives
of Alexandra who have been ordered to live apart in
separate hostels what family life is to them.

Mr. Janson went on to say 'The White man is here to
defend his own identity...' The scandal of the destruc-
tion of all family housing in Alexandra and the policy
of the Government in deciding which families will
be resettled to family accommodation and which will
be ruthlessly torn apart makes one feel that such a
'white' identity is not worth defending."

BOX A3
August to October 1975

"The Black Sash has always stated quite categorically that no amount of cosmetic action can remove the injustice and discrimination. inherent in the pass laws. We have always maintained that to control the lives of the majority of our citizens through a system which demands that every black person must have a permit to be where he wishes to be and to do the ordinary things which all people desire to do and which denies all freedom of movement to millions of people, is so evil that it is totally unacceptable."

BOX A3
February 1975 to January 1976

"The percentage of cases which were successfully con-
cluded has again risen slightly from 22% to 22.4%....
We sometimes doubt the value of keeping records of
successful appeals or applications because it remains
iniquitous that citizens of our country should require
permits to be where they are, to live with their families and to work at all. It is not much of a success
that a woman gets a permit to live with her husband
when her fundamental human RIGHT to do so, without let
or hindrance, remains unrecognized."

Box A3
1976 OPPRESSION AND OFFICIAL SECRECY

"Every year, with monotonous regularity, the Black
Sash annual reports state that the law and the administration of the pass laws has once again become more
severe and more rigid in application. The Johannesburg
Advice Office has not been able to isolate one single
instance in the past year where things have improved,
but constantly finds administrative procedures and actions which are making the oppressive system worse and
life more difficult than it has ever been before… This
fact is greatly aggravated by the habits of secrecy
which the Government and administration has adopted."

Reports on individual cases here are peppered with exclamation points
[!] commenting on the bureaucratic double binds people face, and
personal notes saying things like "I really must get X to let me type her
letters!" and "Y will have a garden tea on Saturday 13th of September.
Members promise to support this." The divide between the individuals
catalogued here makes itself known in several registers.

"Mr ████████████████████████████████: On
Aug. 11th Mr M was returning from the station. The riot
police arrived. The children started running to them
- police started shooting, a bullet <u>shot his eye out</u>
[underlined in original handwriting. A ^ here adds: "he was"] also
shot in arm & side."

In the margins of this page, near "shot his eye out" are doodles of flowers
and pretty little tea cups.

Black Sash Report for April 1984

	Old Cases	New Cases	
Permit problems	43	72	
Contract workers	14	25	
Squatters	4	15	
Squatters to tell of shack demolitions	-	25	
U.I.F. problems	5	16	
Miscellaneous	48	44	
TOTALS	114	197	311

Box A4
MINUTES, CIRCULARS, LETTERS
1986-88

Black Sash Advice Office Annual Report 1984

On Crossroads and KTC areas: "The land in these areas is entirely covered with shacks and plastic shelters housing tens of thousands of people." (4)

"The Crossroads camp started 1984 in a state of warfare and tension and has ended it in much the same way." (4)

"A total of 82 people reported that their shacks had been burnt." (5)

"████████████ is a pain. Got rid of him with great difficulty. Now wonder he has problems. Shack demolished. Poor guy. But he needn't blame me!"

"Mrs R was referred to us by the attorney acting on her behalf. Her husband was taken from their house in Old Crossroads by the 'witdoeks' in June last year and they allegedly handed him over to a particular warrant officer and held him at Gugulethu Police Station. This police station (and all the others in the area) has no record of him ever being held there. The security police have no trace of him in detention. He has disappeared. _It is very difficult to know what to say to a wife in this position._"

████████████████ - Fears of eviction, valid.
████████████████ - Divorced woman- letter to Mr. ████
████ re. accommodation.
████████████████ - Divorced, evicted.
████████████████ - Wife quarreled with neighbours and
they were treated as informers - house set on fire.
████████████████ -Permit problem.
████████████████ - Wage dispute.
████████████████ - Wage dispute.
███████████████████████████ - No book, but wants to
work here. Advised to go back to Lady ████ [ck spell-
ing] and legalize his life.
████████████████ - endorsed out

On and on. Dozens of names followed simply by "endorsed out." Hundreds and hundreds of people sent away from the homes. Pages and pages of short stories about peoples' lives. One minute, they all begin to resemble each other. And then, again, they don't.

1976:

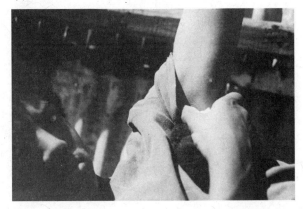

The Department of Plural Relations (Formerly Bantu Affairs)

"The work of the Advice Office springs from the extra burden of laws which apply only to blacks (formerly known as Natives, then as Africans or Bantu depending on the background and now officially Blacks (in preference to Plurals) (1)

"The Government approach, consistent with their entire handling of "Plurals," is to sweep as many as possible of the unemployed (or illegally employed) tidily out of sight (3).

In the 70s, the government, in an effort to get away from the derogatory term "Bantu," began using the term "plural relations" in order to acknowledge the plurality of constituents. Inevitably, some began referring to its "charges" as "plurals." Desmond Tutu once said, "Presumably now we (blacks) were plurals, one of whom would be that very odd thing, a singular plural."

BC 1020 (Advice Office Collection)
A9.Athlone Advice Office Annual Reports 1964-74

"People will always have problems, but those brought to us demonstrate a shameful state of affairs, laws which push men, women, and children around as if they were inanimate and inferior goods, best kept out of sight when not immediately useful. The shame of living with these laws is on us all. There can be no rest in South Africa until her people are treated as people."

In the margin of my own notebook here are notes about On Kawara's minimalist archival art and former South African artist Marlene Dumas' multi-racial portraits. Both artists' work encountered in the library while taking a break. On Kawara has a series called "The Today Paintings" begun in 1966. Each one is a small rectangular canvas with the date it was made depicted in white on a dark monochromatic background. Each one is archivaly boxed with a newspaper clipping from that day. A series of mementos that seem to document the documentary urge itself—an urge to save history that is at once absurd and crucial. Each is unique and yet they are all only marginally different from one another. The Marlene Dumas portraits are a series of watercolor heads painted from photographs, not from life. There are dozens of them. The tonal similarities, the range of apparent, yet ambiguous, ethnicities, even the expressions emphasize both their tender resemblances and their vital differences.

BC 1020 (Advice Office Collection)
A9.Athlone Advice Office Annual Reports 1964-74

"The Advice Office offers Africans and their employers and friends an opportunity to discuss their particular individual problems freely. The background to these problems is well known to be a network of laws designed to keep our cities "white on top" and applied with everyday cruelty, because they are indeed laws and cruel laws can hardly be administered with kindness. It is cruel to keep people away from the only places where they can earn their living and it is cruel to separate husbands and wives, parents and children."

"Too often, all the Office can offer is a sympathetic hearing. But not a week goes by without some considerable success for someone – a job which was lost regained, and with it the right to continue earning a living (even if slender)... such 'full' successes are not very many, but at least half the people who come for help do benefit to some extent. A communication blockage is oiled, a welfare officer undertakes to see someone, a short extension of a permit is granted... On the reverse side of the coin, close study of Advice Office records shows that very often 'the end of the story' was never told."

if you activate parabolas of paint, a concrete floor can switch the drips to semaphore a disappearance subject to a kiss my apparatus lacks ink enough for all this confused back and forth of black on white exclusion and desire, (lingual and eclipsed), weak documents of history and affection's oscillation wreak a politic reminder that the self, while of no matter, still clings like a baby despite fond exhumations where butcher string dangles from a rafter, stuck in looping ovals; eggs of time and rupture. As my eldest says, enough science, you already know it never travels the same route twice.

VI. Epilogue

1.

The "articulation between lyric (the force moving) and documentary (record without judgment)" can be a jammed hinge[33] since economies of selection can't help confer some judgment. Maybe, glimpses can restrain the sentence, or open it up by offering something not fully articulated and therefore more conversational, less declarative. A glance is all we'll get of moments far apart. Sight may be "formed by what we see not by what they say," but let's flag the difficult roadwork of knowing what's seen outside of what is said. There are moments, but the car is moving very fast.

2.

Correspondence can only long for equivalence. A letter of "my day," is not possessive and the "day" lasts just as long as any other history we're approaching, "singing through porous time and porous ego. Elusive. Fast moving." Still, the lyric's past seductions make a pretty mirror for the ugliness of corpses.

3.

A song, a day, the real, ugliness of corpses.

4.

This inky line is a coiled blue umbilical cord floating, uterine, attached to a baby who will be born and die or has already. If this line is narrative, won't it float? Is narrative exclusion really always complicit with systematic exclusions from economic and political power? Listen, wistful, one at a time, he said, line up, chronology's bind is the official version. This is a piece of blue onionskin paper inked with the names of the detained and deceased. Bureaucracy and love.

5.

(To *dialogue with the past, not just derive from it.*) Dialogue with Franz Fanon:

I: And flowers?
F: Only if speaking of consequences, harvests, or of a consciousness that, well….
I: blooms?
F: I wouldn't go that far. Flowers aren't the problem, it's the floral that deceives.
I: The decorative?
F: The teacup, the doodle, the lazy reduction, simplification and its symbol, the usual bourgeois claptrap. Let's move on. We're going back-wards. And I don't do angels either.

6.

The two most commonly heard phrases when people talk about "the new South Africa": "the number of new black millionaires" and "neo-liberal capitalism."

7.

but when I gits my Affikin Up
then I know that Whatever personality (sic) I may
possess is simply the collage effect of
too many meaningful documentaries.

—Notes taken at the Kara Walker show at the Metropolitan Museum of Art, NYC 7/4/06

8.

Some strategies from Rosmarie Waldrop:

- "propose a grammar (a society?) in which subject and object function are not fixed, but reversible roles, where there is no hierarchy of main and subordinate clauses, but a fluid and constant alternation."

- "Jabes, like the German romantics, holds that the fragment is our only access to the infinite. I tend to think it is our way of apprehending anything. Our inclusive views are mosaics. And the shards catch light on the cut, the edges give off sparks"

- "glimpses amount to more than their sum, [that] the breaks allow possibility to enter, as Blanchot says, and thought"

- "The blank page is not blank. Whether we are conscious of it or not, we always write on top of a palimpsest. Like many writers, I have foregrounded this awareness of the palimpsest as a method: using, trans-forming, 'translating' parts of other works. It is not a question of linear 'influence' and not just of tradition. It is a way of getting out of myself. Into what? An interaction, a dialog with language, with a whole net of earlier and concurrent texts. Relation. Between."

9.

"Paradoxically, by hanging on to those older selves in new contexts, one makes an example out of oneself and removes the work from the trappings of ideology that surround the individual. I could enact and re-enact this movement through history, going back in time in a personal way but also interrogating the materials of political, cultural, and human encounters rooted in specific places and times."[34]

10.

Maybe nothing can be said and there's no way to say it, maybe words are to be resisted, but silence can also mean a *simple and crass morality.* [shh, shh, doesn't matter, doesn't matter.] Still, I long to give you the world and the void, my love.

Acknowledgments

This book has taken years to research and write. Many, many people have helped along the way. If you think your name should be here, it should. And I thank you. Among those I especially want to acknowledge are:

Friends and colleagues who were at Drake University when I began this project, especially Graham Foust and Joe Lenz. The Drake Humanities Center and the Drake Center for Global Citizenship. The Centre for African Studies at the University of Cape Town and Leslie Marks of the Manuscript and Archives Division of the University of Cape Town Libraries. All of my family in South Africa, especially Marie Grundlingh, who treated me like a daughter, and Geoff Grundlingh who provided invaluable support. Pumla Gobodo-Madikizela and Nomfundo Waleza for their time and patience. Faculty and friends in the English Department at Ohio University. The Ohio University Baker Fund. Generous, astute, and inspiring friends and readers Kristin Prevallet, Leslie Bumstead, Eula Biss, Carla Harryman, Andrew Mossin, Brian Teare, Spring Ulmer, Kass Fleisher, and others. Editors who published portions: David Lazar (who deserves special thanks), Stephanie G'Schwinde, Dinty Moore, Joyelle McSweeney, John Gallaher, and Amber Withycombe. My parents, Neil and Marie Taylor. My children, Max and Emrys, and all their teachers and caregivers, as well as their father, Richard Milner. Stephen Cope (dreams, intellect, faith). And, crucially, thanks to Anna Moschovakis, Matvei Yankelevich and everyone at Ugly Duckling for bringing this book into the world. Thank you all.

Works Cited

Abahlali baseMjondolo. Web. 29 May 2009. http://www.abahlali.org/node/16.

Agamben, Giorgio. *Remnants of Auschwitz; The Witness and the Archive.* Translated by Daniel Heller-Roazen. New York: Zone Books, 2002.

Alcalay, Ammiel. *From the Warring Factions.* Beyond Baroque, 2002.

Allen, John. *Rabble Rouser for Peace: The Authorized Biography of Desmond Tutu.* New York: Free Press, 2006.

Anderson, Benedict. *Imagined Communities.* New York: Verso, 1992.

Benjamin, Walter. "Surrealism: The Last Snapshot of the European Intelligentsia" (1929). *Reflections: Essays, Aphorisms, Autobiographical Writings.* Edited by Peter Demetz. Translated by Edmund Jephcott. New York: Schocken, 1986.

Benjamin, Walter. *Illuminations.* New York: Schocken, 1969.

Bhabha, Homi K. "DissemiNation; time, narrative, and the margins of the modern nation." *Nations and Narration.* Ed. Homi K. Bhabha. London and New York: Routledge, 1990, 292.

Biko, Steve. *I Write What I Like.* Picador Africa, 2004.

Bloch, Ernst. *A Philosophy of the Future.* Translated by J. Cumming. New York: Herder & Herder, 1970.

Borges, Jorge Luis. "The Aleph." Web. 27 Dec. 2009. http://www.phinnweb.org/links/literature/borges /aleph.html.

Breytenbach, Breyten. *The Memory of Birds in Times of Revolution: Essays on Africa.* New York: Harcourt,1996.

Bush, George. "Address to a Joint Session of Congress and the American People" (2001). Web. 27 Dec. 2009. http://georgewbush-whitehouse.archives.gov/ news/releases/2001/09/20010920-8.html.

Butler, Judith and Gayatri Chakravorty Spivak. *Who Sings the Nation State?: Language, Politics, Belonging.* London: Seagull, 2007.

Currie, Mark. *Postmodern Narrative Theory.* New York: Palgrave Macmillan, 1998.

De Certeau, Michel. *The Writing of History.* New York   mbia University Press, 1988.

DuPlessis, Rachel Blau. *The Pink Guitar: Writing as Feminist Practice.* New York: Routledge, 1990.

Fanon, Frantz. *The Wretched of the Earth.* New York: Grove Press, 1963.

Felman, Shoshana and Dori Laub. *Testimony: Crises of Witnessing in Literature, Psychoanalysis and History.* New York: Routledge, 1992.

Fry, Robbie. "The Influences of Nineteenth Century African American Music On The Popular Music Of South Africa." *Black Praxis,* Spring 2004. Web. 27 Dec. 2009. http://www.ohio.edu/aas/blackpraxis/articles.html.

Geoghan, Vincent. *Ernst Bloch.* New York: Routledge, 1996.

Glissant, Edouard. *Poetics of Relation.* Translated by Betsy Wing. Ann Arbor: The University of Michigan Press, 1997.

Gramsci, Antonio. *Selections from the Prison Notebooks.* New York: International Publishers, 1971.

Griffin, Susan. *A Chorus of Stones: The Private Life of War.* New York: Anchor Books, 1992.

Hejinian, Lyn. *A Border Comedy.* New York: Granary Books, 2001.

Jameson, Fredric. "Pleasure: A Political Issue" in *The Ideologies of Theory: Essays 1971-1986.* Vol. 2: *The Syntax of History.* Minneapolis: University of Minnesota Press, 1988.
---. "Third World Literature in the Era of Multinational Capitalism,' Social Text 15 Fall 1986: 86.

Koestenbaum, Wayne. "Darling's Prick." *The Next American Essay.* Edited by John D'Agata. Saint Paul: Graywolf Press, 2003.

Krog, Antjie. *Country of My Skull.* Johannesburg: Random House, 2002.

Leys, Ruth. *From Guilt to Shame: Auschwitz and After.* Princeton: Princeton University Press, 2007.

Lott, Eric. *Love and Theft; Blackface Minstrelsy and the American Working Class.* Oxford: Oxford University Press, 1995.

Mackey, Nathaniel. *Paracritical Hinge: Essays, Talks, Notes, Interviews.* Madison: University of Wisconsin Press, 2005.

Malan, Rian. "In the Jungle." Originally published in *Rolling Stone* magazine. Now available through Cold Type Modern Classics, 2003. Web. 27 Dec. 2009. www.coldtype.net/Assets/pdfs/Jungle.pdf.
---. *My Traitor's Heart: A South African Exile Returns to Face His Country, His Tribe, and His Conscience.* New York: Vintage, 1990.

Marker, Chris. "Sans Soleil." 1983. Film.

Martin, Denis-Constant. *Coon Carnival; New Year in Cape Town, Past, and Present.* Cape Town: David Philip Publishers, 1999.

Minter, William. *Apartheid's Contras: An Inquiry into the roots of War in Angola. And Mozambique.* Johannesburg: Witwatersrand University Press and London: Zed Books, 1994.

Michaels, Walter Benn. "Going Boom" *BookForum* Volume 15, Issue 5, February/March 2009, 51.

Michaels, Walter Benn. *The Shape of the Signifier: 1967 to the End of History.* Princeton: Princeton University Press, 2004.

Oppen, George. *New Collected Poems.* Edited by Michael Davidson. New York: New Directions Press, 2002.

O'Toole, Sean. "Sean O'Toole on the Albino Series." 2003. Web. 27 Dec. 2009.http://www.michaelstevenson.com/contemporary/exhibitions/hugo/albino.htm. Michael Stevenson Gallery, Cape Town.

Ponge, Francis. *Tome Premier.* Paris: Gallimard, 1965.

Rose, Jacqueline. *On Not Being Able to Sleep: Psychoanalysis and the Modern World.* Princeton: Princeton University Press, 2003.

South African History Online. Web. 24 November 2009. http://www.sahistory.org.za/pages/chronology/general/1970s.html.

Swinton, Ernest. *The Defence of Duffer's Drift.* Combined Arms Center Research Library. Web. 5 September 2007. https://www-cgsc.army.mil/carl/resources/csi/Swinton/Swinton.asp.

Sisulu, Elinor. *Walter and Albertina Sisulu: In Our Lifetime.* Claremont, South Africa: David Philip Publishers, 2002.

Walcott, Derek. *Collected Poems.* 1948-1984. Farrar, Strauss, and Giroux, 1987.

End Notes

1. Perhaps this is the aural equivalent of the Borgesian fantasy of the Aleph—a point in space that contains all others (and all times) and in which one can see everything with no overlap or confusion. For Borges, this point bloomed in the basement of a poet using it to write his poem in order to win win a literary prize.

> I arrive now at the ineffable core of my story. And here begins my despair as a writer. All language is a set of symbols whose use among its speakers assumes a shared past. How, then, can I translate into words the limitless Aleph, which my floundering mind can scarcely encompass? Mystics, faced with the same problem, fall back on symbols: to signify the godhead, one Persian speaks of a bird that somehow is all birds; Alanus de Insulis, of a sphere whose center is everywhere and circumference is nowhere; Ezekiel, of a four-faced angel who at one and the same time moves east and west, north and south. (Not in vain do I recall these inconceivable analogies; they bear some relation to the Aleph.) Perhaps the gods might grant me a similar metaphor, but then this account would become contaminated by literature, by fiction. Really, what I want to do is impossible, for any listing of an endless series is doomed to be infinitesimal. In that single gigantic instant I saw millions of acts both delightful and awful; not one of them occupied the same point in space, without overlapping or transparency. What my eyes beheld was simultaneous, but what I shall now write down will be successive, because language is successive. Nonetheless, I'll try to recollect what I can. (Borges, "The Aleph")

2. Throughout the 1980s South Africa continued to foment war in Angola and Mozambique. "For the most part, the killing went unremarked.... these two conflicts are among the prime examples of 'freedom-fighter' insurgencies celebrated by the international right wing in the last decade of the Cold War. Angola and Mozambique feature a complex interplay of internal, regional and global factors that refuse to fit simple models of wars between nation-states or of purely internal civil wars. State and non-state actors both played active roles." Minter (1-2)

3. Namibia was occupied by South Africa since South Africa invaded German South West Africa in 1915. After WWII, the UN stated that the League of Nations mandate remained valid and requested Namibia be placed under a trusteeship. South Africa resisted this and after 1948 the Nationalists allowed white settlers there to elect members of parliament to the South African government. Namibia didn't gain its independence until March 21, 1990.

4. Homi Bhabha speaks of the nation as "a form of living that is more complex than 'community'; more symbolic than 'society'; more connotative than 'country'; less patriotic than patrie; more rhetorical than the reason of state; more mythological than ideology; less homogeneous than hegemony; less centered than the citizen; more collective than 'the subject'; more psychic than civility; more hybrid in the articulation of cultural differences and identifications–gender, race or class–than can be represented in any hierarchical or binary structuring of social antagonism." (Homi K. Bhaba. "DissemiNation; time, narrative, and the margins of the modern nation.")

5. Breyten Breytenbach. *The Memory of Birds in Times of Revolution: Essays on Africa* (6)

6. Frantz Fanon. "The Pitfalls of National Consciousness." (166)

7. All references to The Black Sash archival material come from research I did in the archives housed at The University of Cape Town in 2004 and 2005. The university now maintains a digital guide to the collection at http://www.lib.uct.ac.za/blacksash/. The archives require that researches protect the anonymity of individuals mentioned in the archives, so all original names have been substituted with pseudonyms.

8. Bill Ashcroft, Gareth Griffiths and Helen Tiffin. *The Empire Writes Back*. London: Routledge, 1989. 149. On Wilson Harris, the authors write, "Harris sees language as the key to these transformations. Language must be altered, its power to lock in fixed beliefs and attitudes must be exposed, and words and concepts "freed" to associate in new ways. There are, he points out, two kinds of relationship to the past—one which derives from the past, and one which is a dialogue with the past."

9. White South African author Breyten Breytenbach, who was jailed as a terrorist for his anti-apartheid activism, famously referred to himself as an "albino terrorist." While his appropriation of the term albino may be problematic vis-a-vis the albino community, naming himself "albino" meant he could both disavow and emphasize his whiteness.

10., 11., 12. Sean O'Toole. "Sean O'Toole on the Albino Series."

13. Rian Malan. *My Traitor's Heart: A South African Exile Returns to Face His Country, His Tribe, and His Conscience*. (28)

14. For more on how Solomon Linda was robbed of possibly as much as $15 million dollars for his song, "Mbube" (also known as "Wimoweh" and "The Lion Sleeps tonight"), see Rian Malan's "In the Jungle." An exposé originally published in Roll-

ing Stone magazine and now available through Cold Type Modern Classics, 2003 at www.coldtype.net/Assets/pdfs/Jungle.pdf.

15. Throughout this essay, I have relied heavily on Eric Lott's excellent book, *Love and Theft; Blackface Minstrelsy and the American Working Class*. On page 147, Lott writes, "Jameson argues [that] the dissolution of the subject in a paroxysm of threatened menace constitutes one way of transforming 'sheer horror' into 'libidinal gratification.'" For Jameson's exploration of this, see "Pleasure: A Political Issue" in *The Ideologies of Theory: Essays 1971-1986. Vol. 2: The Syntax of History*. (61-74)

16. A kaspir is an armored vehicle that was commonly used under apartheid. The phrase "faire une trou" comes from George Oppen's poem "Route" where he writes, "During the occupation the Germans had declared Alsace a part of Greater Germany. Therefore they had drafted Alsatian men into the German army. Many men, learning in their own way that they were to be called, dug a hole. The word became a part of the language: faire une trou..." George Oppen. *New Collected Poems*. Ed. Michael Davidson. New York: New Directions, 2002. 195.

17. Steve Biko. *I Write What I Like* (98-99)

18. Ballantine, cited in Fry, Robbie. "The Influences of Nineteenth Century African American Music On The Popular Music Of South Africa" *Black Praxis*, Spring 2004. Fry also reports, "Although white minstrel troupes were successful, it was African American troupes that had the largest impact on the music of South Africa. In the 1870s, black troupes began to tour South Africa. Their shows differed from the shows of their white counterparts in that they included spirituals in addition to traditional minstrel songs." Fry quotes Angela Impay who says, "Orpheus Mcadoo and his Virginia Jubilee Singers toured South Africa extensively from 1890, inspiring the formation of numerous Black South African groups whose imitation of crude Blackface troupes, song repertoire and musical instruments signaled notions of cultural progress and self improvement" (Impay, 2). Fry also notes the impact these musical styles had on South African choral music known as isicathamiya, including that of Solomon Linda. Fry writes, "Orpheus Mcadoo's influence is obvious in Linda's music, which contains elements of both spirituals and the minstrel stage. When listening to the recording of "Mbube," one instantly recognizes that the banjo is the piece's primary instrument. This indicates a direct influence from the minstrel show. Another connection with the minstrel show is "Mbube's" Western harmonic structure of I-IV-I -V7. This dominant and tonic relationship is similar to that of nineteenth century American popular music. In addition, the singing style is reminiscent of the vocal qualities used in traditional slave songs. Web. 2007. http://www.ohiou.edu/aas/blackpraxis/ article.robbie1.html. 27 Dec. 2009. http://www.ohio.edu/aas/blackpraxis/articles.html.

19. Denis-Constant Martin. *Coon Carnival; New Year in Cape Town, Past, and Present.* (77)

20. Martin. (9)

21. Martin. (80)

22. Martin. (79)

23. "Syncopation." Wikipedia. Cites Peter van der Merwe. *Origins of the Popular Style: The Antecedents of Twentieth-Century Popular Music.* Oxford: Clarendon Press, 1989. 128 Web. 27 Dec. 2009. http://en.wikipedia.org/wiki/Syncopation

24. Martin. (40)

25. Lott. (148)

26. Lott (148-150)

27. Lott. (115)

28. Lott. (124)

29. Official Lyrics of the South African National Anthem. English translation:
God bless Africa,
Lift her horn on high,
Hear our prayers.
God bless us
Who are Your people.

God save our nation,
End wars and strife.
South Africa.

Ringing out from our blue heavens,
from our deep seas breaking round;
Over everlasting mountains
Where the echoing crags resound.

30. Black Sash Archives. University of Cape Town. UCT, BS, A9, Annual Report 77-78. 2.

31. This information is taken practically verbatim from http://www.sahistory.org.za/

pages/chronology/general/1970s.html and is supplemented with information from Walter and Albertina Sisulu by Elinor Sisulu, Albertina Sisulu. 337.

32. Letter from Stephen Cope, 2005 or 2006. "I tend, of course, to be drawn more towards the nomadic and centrifugal rather than to consolidation. Perhaps, that is, not to 'identity' politics but a legitimate politics of 'difference' that's not mere Derridean play. Walcott, then, countered by Braithewaite's 'broken ground' or 'skipped stones' (a la archipelago). And yes, 'guilt,' as you write, in itself is far less productive than despair. You, of course, aren't a nation (nor an island, or continent... but perhaps nonetheless a cosmos.) yr lv"

33. I'm thinking of the essay "Paracritical Hinge" by Nathaniel Mackey. Mackey writes, "Hinge's work as a verb highlights contingency, haunted by tenuousness and risk, an intransitive creaking well worth bearing in mind. The coinage wants to suggest that improvisation, the pursuit of new expressivity, whether musical or literary, is an operation best characterized by the prefix para-, an activity supplemental to more firmly established disciplines and dispositions, an activity that hinges on a near but divergent identity with given disciplines and dispositions."

34. Ammiel Alcalay. *From the Warring Factions.* (177)

Colophon

This book was designed and typeset by goodutopian and printed in an edition of 1,000 by McNaughton & Gunn in Saline, MI. Covers were printed by Polyprint Design in New York City.

Ugly Duckling Presse is a 501(c)(3) not-for-profit publishing collective based in Brooklyn, NY, that specializes in poetry, translation, lost literature, aesthetics, and books by artists.

This book is part of UDP's Dossier Series, which was created in 2008 to expand the formal scope of the Presse. Dossier books don't share a single genre or form but an investigative impulse. For more information about UDP and the Dossier Series, visit www.uglyducklingpresse.org.